HIGH SCHOOL MATHEMATICS AT WORK

ESSAYS AND

EXAMPLES FOR

THE EDUCATION OF

ALL STUDENTS

MATHEMATICAL SCIENCES EDUCATION BOARD
CENTER FOR SCIENCE, MATHEMATICS, AND ENGINEERING EDUCATION
NATIONAL RESEARCH COUNCIL

NATIONAL ACADEMY PRESS
WASHINGTON, D.C. 1998

NATIONAL ACADEMY PRESS • 2101 Constitution Avenue, NW • Washington, DC 20418

NOTICE: The project that is the subject of this report was approved by the Governing Board of the National Research Council, whose members are drawn from the councils of the National Academy of Sciences, the National Academy of Engineering, and the Institute of Medicine. The members of the committee responsible for the report were chosen for their special competences and with regard for appropriate balance.

The National Research Council (NRC) is the operating arm of the National Academies Complex, which includes the National Academy of Sciences, the National Academy of Engineering, and the Institute of Medicine. The National Research Council was organized in 1916 by the National Academy of Sciences to associate the broad community of science and technology with the Academy's purposes of furthering knowledge and providing impartial advice to the federal government. Functioning in accordance with general policies determined by the Academy, the Council has become the principal operating agency of both the National Academy of Sciences and the National Academy of Engineering in providing services to the government, the public, and the scientific and engineering communities. The Council is administered jointly by both Academies and the Institute of Medicine. Dr. Bruce Alberts, President of the National Academy of Sciences, and Dr. William Wulf, President of the National Academy of Engineering, also serve as chairman and vice chairman, respectively, of the National Research Council.

The Center for Science, Mathematics, and Engineering Education (CSMEE) was established in 1995 to provide coordination of all the National Research Council's education activities and reform efforts for students at all levels, specifically those in kindergarten through twelfth grade, undergraduate institutions, school-to-work programs, and continuing education. The Center reports directly to the Governing Board of the National Research Council.

The Mathematical Sciences Education Board was established in 1985 to provide a continuing national capability to assess the status and quality of education in the mathematical sciences and is concerned with excellence in education for all students at all levels. The Board reports directly to the Governing Board of the National Research Council.

Development, publication, and dissemination of this report were supported by a grant from the Pew Charitable Trusts. Any opinions, findings, or recommendations expressed in this report are those of the authors and do not necessarily reflect the views of the Pew Charitable Trusts.

Library of Congress Cataloging-in-Publication Data

High school mathematics at work : essays and examples for the
education of all students / Mathematical Sciences Education Board.
    p. cm.
   Includes bibliographical references and index.
   ISBN 0-309-06353-1 (pbk.)
   1. Mathematics—Study and teaching (Secondary)—United States. I.
National Research Council (U.S.). Mathematical Sciences Education
Board.
   QA13.H54 1998
510'.71'273—ddc21

                                     98-19669

Additional copies of this report may be purchased from the National Academy Press, 2101 Constitution Avenue, NW, Lock Box 285, Washington, DC 20055. (800) 624-6242 or (202) 334-3313 (in the Washington Metropolitan Area). This report is also available online at http://www.nap.edu.

Printed in the United States of America

HIGH SCHOOL MATHEMATICS AT WORK REVIEWERS

This report has been reviewed by individuals chosen for their diverse perspectives and technical expertise, in accordance with procedures approved by the NRC's Report Review Committee. The purpose of this independent review is to provide candid and critical comments that will assist the authors and the NRC in making the published report as sound as possible and to ensure that the report meets institutional standards for objectivity, evidence, and responsiveness to the study charge. The content of the review comments and draft manuscript remain confidential to protect the integrity of the deliberative process. We wish to thank the following individuals for their participation in the review of this report:

George Campbell Jr.
President and CEO, NACME, Inc.,
    New York, NY

Arthur Eisenkraft
Science Coordinator, Bedford Public Schools,
    Bedford, NY

Jane D. Gawronski
Superintendent, Escondido Union High School
    District, Escondido, CA

Cindy Hannon
State Mathematics Specialist, Maryland State
    Department of Education

Harry Kesten
Professor of Mathematics, Cornell University,
    Ithaca, NY

Ron Latanision
Chairman, MIT Council on Primary and
    Secondary Education, Professor of Material
    Science and Engineering, Massachusetts
    Institute of Technology, Cambridge, MA

Douglas H. O'Roark
Mathematics Teacher, Lincoln Park High
    School, Chicago, IL

Diane Resek
Professor of Mathematics, San Francisco
    State University, San Francisco, CA

Judah L. Schwartz
Professor of Education, Harvard University,
    and Emeritus Professor, Engineering
    Science & Education, Massachusetts
    Institute of Technology, Cambridge, MA

While the individuals listed above have provided many constructive comments and suggestions, responsibility for the final content of this report rests solely with the authoring committee and the NRC.

Foreword: Mathematics for a Modern Age

Zell Miller
Governor of Georgia

Now more than ever, our daily lives are directly affected by mathematics. I'm not just talking about the grades students get or how many mathematics classes they have to take. I'm talking about answering the phone, faxing a document, or driving a car. I'm talking about buying medicine for your family, building a house, and listening to music. Mathematics has also helped bring us things that indirectly affect us, like the discoveries of DNA, weather patterns, and how to use light as a surgical tool. It has helped us walk on the moon, create microchips, and transmit images across thousands of miles. With mathematics, we design models to test our ideas and refine them, from nerve impulses to human behavior, volcanoes to food. Mathematics is everywhere. But mathematics has always been around, and the concepts it uses have always helped us.

So why is mathematics so much more important to our lives now than it was then? Years ago, in the eras of the abacus or slide rule, information took a lot longer to sort through, but now it is easy to chart a course, assay a risk, or compare statistics. Information is more abundant than ever. You can find answers about everything from world politics to school lunches almost as soon as you think of the questions.

This new speed of access to volumes of information obviously brings good things—like better medical information, better building materials, and more diverse options in business and education. The down side to all of this is that as easily as there can be information, there can be misuse of information.

So what does this mean for our children? More than ever, they need to be mathematically savvy. Learning to think and reason mathematically is the only way our children can be sure that they are in control, not *being controlled*.

More practically, almost every job these days requires at least some elementary understanding of mathematics. In fact, many of the jobs that keep our country competitive and successful in the global market are jobs that require more than basic mathematics comprehension. Not that everyone needs to be able to program a computer or predict the stock market, but with the vastly increased speed of statistical calculation (and manipulation) and easier and faster global communication, our children need to know what a number means, where it came from, and how best to judge its veracity.

As the Governor of Georgia, I take all of this pretty seriously. I know the importance of bringing businesses to my state to create jobs for Georgians. The world, however, is their marketplace; to be healthy, competitive, and economically secure, our citizens must understand mathematics. They need to become comfortable with the notion of mathematics as a tool for life.

GOVERNOR ZELL MILLER was elected Governor of the state of Georgia in 1990. Since taking office, his love of teaching and commitment to education has resulted in one of the most ambitious agendas to improve public education in this century. Governor Miller's public career includes service at virtually every level of government: as mayor, as a member of the state senate, as lieutenant governor, and now as Governor. He is currently Chairman of the Education Commission of the States. He has also chaired the Southern Governors' Association, the Appalachian Regional Commission, and the Council of State Governments. Governor Miller keynoted the 1992 Democratic National Convention in New York and chaired the Platform Drafting Committee for the 1996 Democratic National Convention in Chicago.

Acknowledgments

For over ten years the Mathematical Sciences Education Board (MSEB) has worked to support the improvement of mathematics education. The work of the Board becomes visible largely through publications, beginning with *Everybody Counts* (1989) and *Reshaping School Mathematics* (1990). *High School Mathematics at Work* builds on this prior work. Like *Measuring Up* (1992), it contains student tasks; like *Mathematical Preparation of the Technical Work Force* (1995), it highlights the mathematics needed for careers.

High School Mathematics at Work was developed through the efforts of more people than can be named individually here. We gratefully acknowledge the generous financial support of the Pew Charitable Trusts, and thank both Robert Schwartz for his special encouragement with this project when he was Director of their Education Programs, as well as Janet Kroll for her continuing interest and support as our program officer.

The project was launched as a 12th grade sequel to *Measuring Up* through the initiative of Linda P. Rosen. The MSEB first envisioned that this sequel would illuminate some features of high quality high school mathematics teaching and learning through standards-based assessment tasks. The growing interest in school-to-work issues, however, led to our giving this theme major prominence. With this new focus, Lynn Arthur Steen and Susan Forman designed the project, secured funding, collected mathematical examples, commissioned essays, and worked with the Task Force, first as members of the MSEB staff and later as consultants. We also thank Daniel Goroff for his leadership during a period of staff transition.

Examples of mathematical tasks were solicited over a period of two years from a wide variety of sources, as described in Appendix A. From the hundreds of examples that were contributed, the Task Force selected about two dozen for inclusion, wrote first drafts of those mathematical examples, and identified essay topics and authors. The resulting collection of examples and essays was molded into its current form by Bradford Findell, serving as editor, under the guidance of Glenda Lappan, Alan Schoenfeld, and Harvey Keynes, with the assistance of Cathy Kessel, and with substantial input from Deborah Ball, Sadie Bragg, Gail Burrill, Shari Coston, Shelley Ferguson, Melvin George, Rick Jennings, Jim Leitzel, Tony Martinez, Pamela Matthews, Patrick McCray, and Jack Price.

Of course, no project of this size could ever come to completion without the contributions of support staff. Thanks especially to Sharon O'Donnell for her help collecting the essays and examples and to Catherine Bell and Doug Sprunger for their help with the review process. We must also thank Sally Stanfield, Linda Humphrey, and the staff at the National Academy Press for their support and patience with the complex evolution of this project.

HYMAN BASS, CHAIRMAN
Mathematical Sciences Education Board

REFERENCES

National Research Council. (1989). *Everybody counts: A report to the nation on the future of mathematics education*. Washington, DC: National Academy Press.

National Research Council. (1990). *Reshaping school mathematics: A philosophy and framework for curriculum*. Washington, DC: National Academy Press.

National Research Council. (1993). *Measuring up: Prototypes for mathematics assessment*. Washington, DC: National Academy Press.

National Research Council. (1995). *Mathematical preparation of the technical work force*. Washington, DC: National Academy Press.

Additional thanks for the many efforts and suggestions offered by the following people:

Jennifer Bemis, John Bishop, Judy Estep, Jim Fey, Carol Findell, Kent Findell, Irene Gable, Jim Gates, Mary Hornyak, Ramona Irvin, Jay Labov, Patrice Legro, Diane Mann, Bob Naismith, Harold Pratt, Kirsten Sampson, Harold Shoen, Kevin Sullivan, Jan Tuomi, Phil Wagreich, Tina Winters, and Judi Zawojewski.

Table of Contents

PART FOUR

IMPLICATIONS FOR TEACHING AND TEACHER EDUCATION

PART FIVE

EPILOGUE • 157

APPENDIXES

INDEX • 171

Introduction

Society's technological, economic, and cultural changes of the last 50 years have made many important mathematical ideas more relevant and accessible in work and in everyday life. As examples of mathematics proliferate, the mathematics education community is provided with both a responsibility and an opportunity. Educators have a responsibility to provide a high-quality mathematics education for all of our students. A recent report of the National Academy of Sciences (NAS) entitled *Preparing for the 21st Century: The Education Imperative* (National Research Council [NRC], 1997) neatly summarizes this point:

> ... today, an understanding of science, mathematics, and technology is very important in the workplace. As routine mechanical and clerical tasks become computerized, more and more jobs require high-level skills that involve critical thinking, problem solving, communicating ideas to others and collaborating effectively. Many of these jobs build on skills developed through high-quality science, mathematics, and technology education. Our nation is unlikely to remain a world leader without a better-educated workforce. (p. 1)

These economic and technological changes also present an opportunity for providing that high-quality education. Specifically, there is rich mathematics in workplace applications and in everyday life that can contribute to the school curriculum. Thus, today's world not only calls for increasing connection between mathematics and its applications, but also provides compelling examples of mathematical ideas in everyday and workplace settings. These examples can serve to broaden the nation's mathematics education programs to encompass the dual objectives of preparing students for the worlds of work and of higher education. Furthermore, such programs can provide students with the flexibility to return to higher education whenever appropriate in their career paths. By illustrating the commonalities among the mathematical expectations for college, for work, and for everyday life, and by illustrating sophisticated uses of mathematics taught in high schools as well as in community colleges, this document aims to offer an expanded vision of mathematics. Mathematics based in the workplace and in everyday life can be good mathematics for everyone.

High School Mathematics at Work is a collection of essays and illustrative tasks from workplace and everyday contexts that suggest ways to strengthen the mathematical education of all students. The essays are written by a wide range of individuals who have thought deeply about mathematics education and about the futures of today's students, from mathematics educators to business leaders, from mathematicians to educational researchers, from curriculum developers to policy makers. The essays and tasks in *High School Mathematics at Work* not only underscore the points made in *The Education Imperative* (NRC, 1997), but also begin to explore connections between academic mathematics and mathematics for work and life.

As a step toward examining ways in which our schools and colleges can better serve the needs of both academic and vocational education, the National Research Council (NRC) of the National Academy of Sciences hosted a workshop in 1994 that resulted in a report entitled *Mathematical Preparation of the Technical Work Force* (NRC, 1995). Participants discussed questions such as

- How can mathematics content and technical applications of mathematics be integrated into educational programs?

- Should algebra continue to be the "critical filter" used to determine whether or not students will be admitted into youth apprenticeship programs?

- Is the mathematics included in technical education programs consistent with emerging educational and occupational skills standards?

- Is it possible (or desirable) to design a core mathematics curriculum for the high school and community college levels that prepares students both for further formal education and for immediate employment in the technical work force? (p. 6)

High School Mathematics at Work continues discussion of these questions, and considers in particular how workplace and everyday mathematics can enrich mathematics teaching and learning.

Though the nominal mathematical content of this volume is high school mathematics, consideration of the above issues will lead to implications for colleges as well. For example, some two-year colleges have moved toward programs that include contextual learning and work-based experiences to enhance academic learning, often through articulated 2+2 partnerships that combine two years of course-work in high school with two years at a community college. The movement toward work-based learning has gained momentum in recent years through the School-to-Work Opportunities Act of 1994, administered jointly by the Departments of Education and Labor, and through the Advanced Technological Education program at the National Science Foundation. Both programs emphasize high academic expectations and require strong connections among schools, two-year colleges, businesses, and industry. By bringing these issues to the attention of the broader college and school communities, and by promoting higher mathematical expectations for all students, this document might provide an opportunity for schools and colleges to reconsider the mathematics courses before calculus, perhaps leading to new conceptualizations of their remedial, developmental, and "liberal arts" courses.

Fundamentally, *High School Mathematics at Work* is about mathematics. Its view of mathematics and mathematics learning recognizes a potential symbiotic relationship between concrete and abstract mathematics, each contributing to the other, enhancing their joint richness and power. This view is not new. Historically, much mathematics originated from attempts to solve problems from science and engineering. On the other hand, solutions to many problems from science and engineering have been based on creative ways of applying some mathematics that until then had no known applications. Mathematics can help solve problems, and complex workplace problems can help stimulate the creation of new mathematics.

Embracing this connected view of mathematics requires more than addressing content issues. In this document, the essays and tasks are organized according to four themes, each considering a different aspect of the many challenges involved in creating an enriched mathematics education for students. Each theme is introduced by an overview that provides a context for and a summary of the essays and tasks that follow. The first theme, *Connecting Mathematics with Work and Life*, sets the stage for the document as a whole, examining why and how "real world problems" can be used to enhance the learning of mathematics. With that premise, the remaining themes emphasize implications for various components of the educational system. *The Roles of Standards and Assessments* highlights the roles of standards and assessments in maintaining and also changing a vision of mathematics education. *Curricular Considerations* explores ways of designing curricula that attend to the needs of a diverse citizenry. Finally, *Implications for Teaching and Teacher Education* underscores the background and support teachers must have to respond to the needs of today's students.

Many of the issues raised by these essays are quite complex; no single essay provides a definitive resolution for any of these issues, and in fact, on some matters, some of the essayists disagree. Collectively, these essays point toward a vision of mathematics education that simultaneously considers the needs of all students. *High School Mathematics at Work*, however, unlike many documents produced by the National Research Council, is not a consensus document. The intent of this document is to point out some mathematical possibilities that are provided by today's world and to discuss some of the issues involved—not to resolve the issues, but to put forward some individual and personal perspectives that may contribute to the discussion.

Under each theme, the essays are accompanied by several tasks that illustrate some of the points raised in those essays, though many of the tasks could appropriately fit under several of the themes. The tasks serve as examples of where today's world can provide good contexts for good mathematics. They never were intended to represent, or even suggest, a full menu of high school mathematics. They provide possibilities for teaching. They exemplify central mathematical ideas and simultaneously convey the explanatory power of mathematics to help us make sense of the world around us. This book offers an existence proof: one can make connections between typical high school mathematics content and important problems from our everyday lives. And, it makes an important point: that the mathematics we learn in the classroom can and should help us to deal with the situations we encounter in our everyday lives. But *High School Mathematics at Work* is not only about relevance and utility. The mathematics involved is often generalizable; it often has aesthetic value, too. Mathematics can be beautiful, powerful, and useful. We hope you will discover all three of these virtues in some of the examples.

At a time when analysts of the Third International Mathematics and Science Study (TIMSS) have characterized the K-12 mathematics curriculum as "a mile wide and an inch deep" (Schmidt, McKnight & Raizen, 1996) this report does not advocate that tasks like the ones in this volume merely augment the curriculum. Rather, it suggests that tasks like these can provide meaningful contexts for important mathematics we already teach, including both well-established topics such as exponential growth and proportional reasoning, as well as more recent additions to the curriculum, such as data analysis and statistics.

Collectively, these essays and tasks explore how mathematics supports careers that are both high in stature and widely in demand. By suggesting ways that mathematics education can be structured to serve the needs of all students, the Mathematical Sciences Education Board (MSEB) hopes to initiate, inform, and invigorate discussions of how and what might be taught to whom. To this end, *High School Mathematics at Work* is appropriate for a broad audience, including teachers, teacher educators, college faculty, parents, mathematicians, curriculum designers, superintendents, school board members, and policy makers—in short, anyone interested in mathematics education. For those who teach mathematics, the essays might provide new ways of thinking about teaching and learning; the tasks might provide ideas for the classroom. For parents, this book can give a sense of how mathematics can be powerful, useful, beautiful, meaningful, and relevant for students. And for those who influence educational policy, this book might motivate a search for curricula with these virtues.

As with all of the recent published work of the MSEB, *High School Mathematics at Work* is meant to be shared by all who care about the future of mathematics education, to serve as a stimulus for further discussion, planning, and action. All those who contributed to this report would be delighted if teachers gave copies to school board members, college faculty gave copies to deans, curriculum developers gave copies to publishers, employers gave copies to policy makers, and so on. Only through continued, broad-based discussion of curricular issues can we implement change and raise our expectations of what students know and are able to do.

REFERENCES

National Research Council. (1995). *Mathematical preparation of the technical work force*. Washington, DC: National Academy Press.

National Research Council. (1997). *Preparing for the 21st century: The education imperative*. Washington, DC: National Academy Press.

Schmidt, W. H., McKnight, C. C., & Raizen, S. A. (1996). *A splintered vision: An investigation of U.S. science and mathematics education*. Dordrecht, The Netherlands: Kluwer Academic Publishers.

PART ONE

Connecting
Mathematics with
Work and Life

OVERVIEW

Mathematics is the key to opportunity. No longer just the language of science, mathematics now contributes in direct and fundamental ways to business, finance, health, and defense. For students, it opens doors to careers. For citizens, it enables informed decisions. For nations, it provides knowledge to compete in a technological community. To participate fully in the world of the future, America must tap the power of mathematics. (NRC, 1989, p. 1)

The above statement remains true today, although it was written almost ten years ago in the Mathematical Sciences Education Board's (MSEB) report *Everybody Counts* (NRC, 1989). In envisioning a future in which all students will be afforded such opportunities, the MSEB acknowledges the crucial role played by formulae and algorithms, and suggests that algorithmic skills are more flexible, powerful, and enduring when they come from a place of meaning and understanding. *This volume takes as a premise that all students can develop mathematical understanding by working with mathematical tasks from workplace and everyday contexts.* The essays in this report provide some rationale for this premise and discuss some of the issues and questions that follow. The tasks in this report illuminate some of the possibilities provided by the workplace and everyday life.

Contexts from within mathematics also can be powerful sites for the development of mathematical understanding, as professional and amateur mathematicians will attest. There are many good sources of compelling problems from within mathematics, and a broad mathematics education will include experience with problems from contexts both within and outside mathematics. The inclusion of tasks in this volume is intended to highlight particularly compelling problems whose context lies outside of mathematics, not to suggest a curriculum.

The operative word in the above premise is "can." The understandings that students develop from any encounter with mathematics depend not only on the context, but also on the students' prior experience and skills, their ways of thinking, their engagement with the task, the environment in which they explore the task—including the teacher, the students, and the tools—the kinds of interactions that occur in that environment, and the system of internal and external incentives that might be associated with the activity. Teaching and learning are complex activities that depend upon evolving and rarely articulated interrelationships among teachers, students, materials, and ideas. No prescription for their improvement can be simple.

This volume may be beneficially seen as a rearticulation and elaboration of a principle put forward in *Reshaping School Mathematics*:

Principle 3: Relevant applications should be an integral part of the curriculum.

Students need to experience mathematical ideas in the context in which they naturally arise—from simple counting and measurement to applications in business and science. Calculators and computers make it possible now to introduce realistic applications throughout the curriculum.

The significant criterion for the suitability of an application is whether it has the potential to engage students' interests and stimulate their mathematical thinking. (NRC, 1990, p. 38)

Mathematical problems can serve as a source of motivation for students if the problems engage students' interests and aspirations. Mathematical problems also can serve as sources of meaning and understanding if the problems stimulate students' thinking. Of course, a mathematical task that is meaningful to a student will provide more motivation than a task that does not make sense. The rationale behind the criterion above is that both meaning and motivation are required. The motivational benefits that can be provided by workplace and everyday problems are worth mentioning, for although some students are aware that certain mathematics courses are necessary in order to gain entry into particular career paths, many students are unaware of how particular topics or problem-solving approaches will have relevance in any workplace. The power of using workplace and everyday problems to teach mathematics lies not so much in motivation, however, for no context by itself will motivate all students. The real power is in connecting to students' thinking.

There is growing evidence in the literature that problem-centered approaches—including mathematical contexts, "real world" contexts, or both—can promote learning of both skills and concepts. In one comparative study, for example, with a high school curriculum that included rich applied problem situations, students scored somewhat better than comparison students on algebraic procedures and significantly better on conceptual and problem-solving tasks (Schoen & Ziebarth, 1998). This finding was further verified through task-based interviews. Studies that show superior performance of students in problem-centered classrooms are not limited to high schools. Wood and Sellers (1996), for example, found similar results with second and third graders.

Research with adult learners seems to indicate that "variation of contexts (as well as the whole task approach) tends to encourage the development of general understanding in a way which concentrating on repeated routine applications of algorithms does not and cannot" (Strässer, Barr, Evans, & Wolf, 1991, p. 163). This conclusion is consistent with the notion that using a variety of contexts can increase the chance that students can show what they know. By increasing the number of potential links to the diverse knowledge and experience of the students, more students have opportunities to excel, which is to say that the above premise can promote equity in mathematics education.

There is also evidence that learning mathematics through applications can lead to exceptional achievement. For example, with a curriculum that emphasizes modeling and applications, high school students at the North Carolina School of Science and Mathematics have repeatedly submitted winning papers in the annual college competition, Mathematical Contest in Modeling (Cronin, 1988; Miller, 1995).

The relationships among teachers, students, curricular materials, and pedagogical approaches are complex. Nonetheless, the literature does supports the premise that workplace and everyday problems *can* enhance mathematical learning, and suggests that if students engage in mathematical thinking, they will be afforded opportunities for building connections, and therefore meaning and understanding.

In the opening essay, Dale Parnell argues that traditional teaching has been missing opportunities for connections: between subject-matter and context, between academic and vocational education, between school and life, between knowledge and application, and between subject-matter disciplines. He suggests that teaching must change if more students are to learn mathematics. The question, then, is how to exploit opportunities for connections between high school mathematics and the workplace and everyday life.

Rol Fessenden shows by example the importance of mathematics in business, specifically in making marketing decisions. His essay opens with a dialogue among employees of a company that intends to expand its business into

Japan, and then goes on to point out many of the uses of mathematics, data collection, analysis, and non-mathematical judgment that are required in making such business decisions.

In his essay, Thomas Bailey suggests that vocational and academic education both might benefit from integration, and cites several trends to support this suggestion: change and uncertainty in the workplace, an increased need for workers to understand the conceptual foundations of key academic subjects, and a trend in pedagogy toward collaborative, open-ended projects. Furthermore, he observes that School-to-Work experiences, first intended for students who were not planning to attend a four-year college, are increasingly being seen as useful in preparing students for such colleges. He discusses several such programs that use work-related applications to teach academic skills and to prepare students for college. Integration of academic and vocational education, he argues, can serve the dual goals of "grounding academic standards in the realistic context of workplace requirements and introducing a broader view of the potential usefulness of academic skills even for entry level workers."

Noting the importance and utility of mathematics for jobs in science, health, and business, Jean Taylor argues for continued emphasis in high school of topics such as algebra, estimation, and trigonometry. She suggests that workplace and everyday problems can be useful ways of teaching these ideas for *all* students.

There are too many different kinds of workplaces to represent even most of them in the classrooms. Furthermore, solving mathematics problems from some workplace contexts requires more contextual knowledge than is reasonable when the goal is to learn mathematics. (Solving some other workplace problems requires more mathematical knowledge than is reasonable in high school.) Thus, contexts must be chosen carefully for their opportunities for sense making. But for students who have knowledge of a workplace, there are opportunities for mathematical connections as well. In their essay, Daniel Chazan and Sandra Callis Bethell describe an approach that creates such opportunities for students in an algebra course for 10th through 12th graders, many of whom carried with them a "heavy burden of negative experiences" about mathematics. Because the traditional Algebra I curriculum had been extremely unsuccessful with these students, Chazan and Bethell chose to do something different. One goal was to help students see mathematics in the world around them. With the help of community sponsors, Chazen and Bethell asked students to look for mathematics in the workplace and then describe that mathematics and its applications to their classmates.

The tasks in Part One complement the points made in the essays by making direct connections to the workplace and everyday life. **Emergency Calls** (p. 42) illustrates some possibilities for data analysis and representation by discussing the response times of two ambulance companies. **Back-of-the-Envelope Estimates** (p. 45) shows how quick, rough estimates and calculations are useful for making business decisions. **Scheduling Elevators** (p. 49) shows how a few simplifying assumptions and some careful reasoning can be brought together to understand the difficult problem of optimally scheduling elevators in a large office building. Finally, in the context of a discussion with a client of an energy consulting firm, **Heating-Degree-Days** (p. 54) illuminates the mathematics behind a common model of energy consumption in home heating.

REFERENCES

Cronin, T. P. (1988). High school students win "college" competition. *Consortium: The Newsletter of the Consortium for Mathematics and Its Applications, 26*, 3, 12.

Miller, D. E. (1995). North Carolina sweeps MCM '94. *SIAM News, 28*(2).

National Research Council. (1989). *Everybody counts: A report to the nation on the future of mathematics education*. Washington, DC: National Academy Press.

National Research Council. (1990). *Reshaping school mathematics: A philosophy and framework for curriculum*. Washington, DC: National Academy Press.

Schoen, H. L. & Ziebarth, S. W. (1998). *Assessment of students' mathematical performance* (A Core-Plus Mathematics Project Field Test Progress Report). Iowa City: Core Plus Mathematics Project Evaluation Site, University of Iowa.

Strässer, R., Barr, G. Evans, J. & Wolf, A. (1991). Skills versus understanding. In M. Harris (Ed.), *Schools, mathematics, and work* (pp. 158-168). London: The Falmer Press.

Wood, T. & Sellers, P. (1996). Assessment of a problem-centered mathematics program: Third grade. *Journal for Research in Mathematics Education, 27*(3), 337-353.

1 Mathematics as a Gateway to Student Success

Dale Parnell
Oregon State University

The study of mathematics stands, in many ways, as a gateway to student success in education. This is becoming particularly true as our society moves inexorably into the technological age. Therefore, it is vital that more students develop higher levels of competency in mathematics.[1]

The standards and expectations for students must be high, but that is only half of the equation. The more important half is the development of teaching techniques and methods that will help all students (rather than just some students) reach those higher expectations and standards. This will require some changes in how mathematics is taught.

Effective education must give clear focus to connecting real life context with subject-matter content for the student, and this requires a more "connected" mathematics program. In many of today's classrooms, especially in secondary school and college, teaching is a matter of putting students in classrooms marked "English," "history," or "mathematics," and then attempting to fill their heads with facts through lectures, textbooks, and the like. Aside from an occasional lab, workbook, or "story problem," the element of contextual teaching and learning is absent, and little attempt is made to connect what students are learning with the world in which they will be expected to work and spend their lives. Often the fragmented information offered to students is of little use or application except to pass a test.

What we do in most traditional classrooms is require students to commit bits of knowledge to memory in isolation from any practical application—to simply take our word that they "might need it later." For many students, "later" never arrives. This might well be called the freezer approach to teaching and learning. In effect, we are handing out information to our students and saying, "Just put this in your mental freezer; you can thaw it out later should you need it." With the exception of a minority of students who do well in mastering abstractions with little contextual experience, students aren't buying that offer. The neglected majority of students see little personal meaning in what they are asked to learn, and they just don't learn it.

I recently had occasion to interview 75 students representing seven different high schools in the Northwest. In nearly all cases, the students were juniors identified as vocational or general education students. The comment of one student stands out as representative of what most of these students told me in one way or another: "I know it's up to me to get an education, but a lot of times school is just so dull and boring. . . . You go to this class, go to that class, study a little of this and a little of that, and nothing connects. . . . I would like to really understand and know the application for what I am learning." Time and again, students were asking, "Why do I have to learn this?" with few sensible answers coming from the teachers.

My own long experience as a community college president confirms the thoughts of these students. In most community colleges today, one-third to one-half of the entering students are enrolled in developmental (remedial) education, trying to make up for what they did not learn in earlier education experiences. A large majority of these students come to the community college with limited mathematical skills and abilities that hardly go beyond adding, subtracting, and multiplying with whole numbers. In addition, the need for remediation is also experienced, in varying degrees, at four-year colleges and universities.

What is the greatest sin committed in the teaching of mathematics today? It is the failure to help students use the magnificent power of the brain to make connections between the following:

- subject-matter content and the context of use;

- academic and vocational education;

- school and other life experiences;

- knowledge and application of knowledge; and

- one subject-matter discipline and another.

Why is such failure so critical? Because understanding the idea of making the connection between subject-matter content and the context of application is what students, at all levels of education, desperately require to survive and succeed in our high-speed, high-challenge, rapidly changing world.

Educational policy makers and leaders can issue reams of position papers on longer school days and years, site-based management, more achievement tests and better assessment practices, and other "hot" topics of the moment, but such papers alone will not make the crucial difference in what students know and can do. The difference will be made when classroom teachers begin to connect learning with real-life experiences in new, applied ways, and when education reformers begin to focus upon learning for meaning.

A student may memorize formulas for determining surface area and measuring angles and use those formulas correctly on a test, thereby achieving the behavioral objectives set by the teacher. But when confronted with the need to construct a building or repair a car, the same student may well be left at sea because he or she hasn't made the connection between the formulas and their real-life application. When students are asked to consider the Pythagorean Theorem, why not make the lesson active, where students actually lay out the foundation for a small building like a storage shed?

What a difference mathematics instruction could make for students if it were to stress the context of application—as well as the content of knowledge—using the problem-solving model over the freezer model. Teaching conducted upon the connected model would help more students learn with their thinking brain, as well as with their memory brain, developing the competencies and tools they need to survive and succeed in our complex, interconnected society.

One step toward this goal is to develop mathematical tasks that integrate subject-matter content with the context of application and that are aimed at preparing individuals for the world of work as well as for postsecondary education. Since many mathematics teachers have had limited workplace experience, they need many good examples of how knowledge of mathematics can be applied to real life situations. The trick in developing mathematical tasks for use in classrooms will be to keep the tasks connected to real life situations that the student will recognize. The tasks should not be just a contrived exercise but should stay as close to solving common problems as possible.

As an example, why not ask students to compute the cost of 12 years of schooling in a public school? It is a sad irony that after 12 years of schooling most students who attend the public schools have no idea of the cost of their schooling or how their education was financed. No wonder that some public schools have difficulty gaining financial support! The individuals being served by the schools have never been exposed to the real life context of who pays for the schools and why. Somewhere along the line in the teaching of mathematics, this real life learning opportunity has been missed, along with many other similar contextual examples.

The mathematical tasks in *High School Mathematics at Work* provide students (and teachers) with a plethora of real life mathematics problems and challenges to be faced in everyday life and work. The challenge for teachers will be to develop these tasks so they relate as close as possible to where students live and work every day.

REFERENCES

Parnell, D. (1985). *The neglected majority*. Washington, DC: Community College Press.
Parnell, D. (1995). *Why do I have to learn this?* Waco, TX: CORD Communications.

NOTE

1. For further discussion of these issues, see Parnell (1985, 1995).

DALE PARNELL is Professor Emeritus of the School of Education at Oregon State University. He has served as a University Professor, College President, and for ten years as the President and Chief Executive Officer of the American Association of Community Colleges. He has served as a consultant to the National Science Foundation and has served on many national commissions, such as the Secretary of Labor's Commission on Achieving Necessary Skills (SCANS). He is the author of the book *The Neglected Majority* which provided the foundation for the federally-funded Tech Prep Associate Degree Program.

2 MARKET LAUNCH

ROL FESSENDEN
L. L. BEAN, INC.

"OK, the agenda of the meeting is to review the status of our launch into Japan. You can see the topics and presenters on the list in front of you. Gregg, can you kick it off with a strategy review?"

"Happy to, Bob. We have assessed the possibilities, costs, and return on investment of opening up both store and catalog businesses in other countries. Early research has shown that both Japan and Germany are good candidates. Specifically, data show high preference for good quality merchandise, and a higher-than-average propensity for an active outdoor lifestyle in both countries. Education, age, and income data are quite different from our target market in the U.S., but we do not believe that will be relevant because the cultures are so different. In addition, the Japanese data show that they have a high preference for things American, and, as you know, we are a classic American company. Name recognition for our company is 14%, far higher than any of our American competition in Japan. European competitors are virtually unrecognized, and other Far Eastern competitors are perceived to be of lower quality than us. The data on these issues are quite clear.

"Nevertheless, you must understand that there is a lot of judgment involved in the decision to focus on Japan. The analyses are limited because the cultures are different and we expect different behavioral drivers. Also, much of the data we need in Japan are simply not available because the Japanese marketplace is less well developed than in the U.S. Drivers' license data, income data, lifestyle data, are all commonplace here and unavailable there. There is little prior penetration in either country by American retailers, so there is no experience we can draw upon. We have all heard how difficult it will be to open up sales operations in Japan, but recent sales trends among computer sellers and auto parts sales hint at an easing of the difficulties.

"The plan is to open three stores a year, 5,000 square feet each. We expect to do $700/square foot, which is more than double the experience of American retailers in the U.S. but 45% less than our stores. In addition, pricing will be 20% higher to offset the cost of land and buildings. Asset costs are approximately twice their rate in the U.S., but labor is slightly less. Benefits are more thoroughly covered by the government. Of course, there is a lot of uncertainty in the sales volumes we are planning. The pricing will cover some of the uncertainty but is still less than comparable quality goods already being offered in Japan.

"Let me shift over to the competition and tell you what we have learned. We have established long-term relationships with 500 to 1000 families in each country. This is comparable to our practice in the U.S. These families do not know they are working specifically with our company, as this would skew their reporting. They keep us appraised of their catalog and shopping experiences, regardless of the company they purchase from. The sample size is large enough to be significant, but, of course, you have to be careful about small differences.

"All the families receive our catalog and catalogs from several of our competitors. They match the lifestyle, income, and education demographic profiles of the people we want to have as customers. They are experienced catalog shoppers, and this will skew their feedback as compared to new catalog shoppers.

"One competitor is sending one 100-page catalog per quarter. The product line is quite narrow—200 products out of a domestic line of 3,000. They have selected items that are not likely to pose fit problems: primarily outerwear and knit shirts, not many pants, mostly men's goods, not women's. Their catalog copy is in Kanji, but the style is a bit stilted we are told, probably because it was written in English and translated, but we need to test this hypothesis. By contrast, we have simply mailed them the same catalog we use in the U.S., even written in English.

"Customer feedback has been quite clear. They prefer our broader assortment by a ratio of 3:1, even though they don't buy most of the products. As the competitors figured, sales are focused on outerwear and knits, but we are getting more sales, apparently because they like looking at the catalog and spend more time with it. Again, we need further testing. Another hypothesis is that our brand name is simply better known.

"Interestingly, they prefer our English-language version because they find it more of an adventure to read the catalog in another language. This is probably a built-in bias of our sampling technique because we specifically selected people who speak English. We do not expect this trend to hold in a general mailing.

"The English language causes an 8% error rate in orders, but orders are 25% larger, and 4% more frequent. If we can get them to order by phone, we can correct the errors immediately during the call.

"The broader assortment, as I mentioned, is resulting in a significantly higher propensity to order, more units per order, and the same average unit cost. Of course, paper and postage costs increase as a consequence of the larger format catalog. On the other hand, there are production efficiencies from using the same version as the domestic catalog. Net impact, even factoring in the error rate, is a significant sales increase. On the other hand, most of the time, the errors cause us to ship the wrong item which then needs to be mailed back at our expense, creating an impression in the customers that we are not well organized even though the original error was theirs.

"Final point: The larger catalog is being kept by the customer an average of 70 days, while the smaller format is only kept on average for 40 days. Assuming—we need to test this—that the length of time they keep the catalog is proportional to sales volumes, this is good news. We need to assess the over-all impact carefully, but it appears that there is a significant population for which an English-language version would be very profitable."

"Thanks, Gregg, good update. Jennifer, what do you have on customer research?"

"Bob, there's far more that we need to know than we have been able to find out. We have learned that Japan is very fad-driven in apparel tastes and fasci-nated by American goods. We expect sales initially to sky-rocket, then drop like a stone. Later on, demand will level out at a profitable level. The graphs on page 3 [Figure 2-1] show demand by week for 104 weeks, and we have assessed several scenarios. They all show a good underlying business, but the uncertainty is in the initial take-off. The best data are based on the Italian fashion boom which Japan experienced in the late 80s. It is not strictly analogous because it revolved around dress apparel instead of our casual and weekend wear. It is, however, the best infor-mation available.

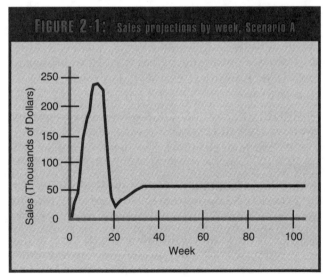

FIGURE 2-1: Sales projections by week, Scenario A

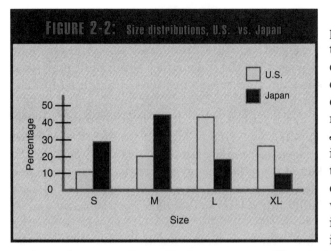

FIGURE 2-2: Size distributions, U.S. vs. Japan

"Our effectiveness in positioning inventory for that initial surge will be critical to our long-term success. There are excellent data—supplied by MITI, I might add—that show that Japanese customers can be intensely loyal to companies that meet their high service expectations. That is why we prepared several scenarios. Of course, if we position inventory for the high scenario, and we experience the low one, we will experience a significant loss due to liquidations. We are still analyzing the long-term impact, however. It may still be worthwhile to take the risk if the 2-year ROI[1] is sufficient.

"We have solid information on their size scales [Figure 2-2]. Seventy percent are small and medium. By comparison, 70% of Americans are large and extra large. This will be a challenge to manage but will save a few bucks on fabric.

"We also know their color preferences, and they are very different than Americans. Our domestic customers are very diverse in their tastes, but 80% of Japanese customers will buy one or two colors out of an offering of 15. We are still researching color choices, but it varies greatly for pants versus shirts, and for men versus women. We are confident we can find patterns, but we also know that it is easy to guess wrong in that market. If we guess wrong, the liquidation costs will be very high.

"Bad news on the order-taking front, however. They don't like to order by phone. . . ."

ANALYSIS

In this very brief exchange among decision-makers we observe the use of many critically important skills that were originally learned in public schools. Perhaps the most important is one not often mentioned, and that is the ability to convert an important business question into an appropriate mathematical one, to solve the mathematical problem, and then to explain the implications of the solution for the original business problem. This ability to inhabit simultaneously the business world and the mathematical world, to translate between the two, and, as a consequence, to bring clarity to complex, real-world issues is of extraordinary importance.

In addition, the participants in this conversation understood and interpreted graphs and tables, computed, approximated, estimated, interpolated, extrapolated, used probabilistic concepts to draw conclusions, generalized from small samples to large populations, identified the limits of their analyses, discovered relationships, recognized and used variables and functions, analyzed and compared data sets, and created and interpreted models. Another very important aspect of their work was that they identified additional questions, and they suggested ways to shed light on those questions through additional analysis.

There were two broad issues in this conversation that required mathematical perspectives. The first was to develop as rigorous and cost effective a data collection and analysis process as was practical. It involved perhaps 10 different analysts who attacked the problem from different viewpoints. The process also required integration of the mathematical learnings of all 10 analysts and translation of the results into business language that could be understood by non-mathematicians.

The second broad issue was to understand from the perspective of the decision-makers who were listening to the presentation which results were most reliable, which were subject to reinterpretation, which were actually judgments not supported by appropriate analysis, and which were hypotheses that truly required more research. In addition, these business people would likely identify synergies in the research that were not contemplated by the analysts. These synergies need to be analyzed to determine if—mathematically— they were real. The most obvious one was where the inventory analysts said that the customers don't like to use the phone to place orders. This is bad news for the sales analysts who are counting on phone data collection to correct errors caused by language problems. Of course, we need more information to know the magnitude—or even the existence—of the problem.

In brief, the analyses that preceded the dialogue might each be considered a mathematical task in the business world:

- A cost analysis of store operations and catalogs was conducted using data from existing American and possibly other operations.

- Customer preferences research was analyzed to determine preferences in quality and life-style. The data collection itself could not be carried out by a high school graduate without guidance, but 80% of the analysis could.

- Cultural differences were recognized as a causes of analytical error. Careful analysis required judgment. In addition, sources of data were identified in the U.S., and comparable sources were found lacking in Japan. A search was conducted for other comparable retail experience, but none was found. On the other hand, sales data from car parts and computers were assessed for relevance.

- Rates of change are important in understanding how Japanese and American stores differ. Sales per square foot, price increases, asset costs, labor costs and so forth were compared to American standards to determine whether a store based in Japan would be a viable business.

- "Nielsen" style ratings of 1000 families were used to collect data. Sample size and error estimates were mentioned. Key drivers of behavior (lifestyle, income, education) were mentioned, but this list may not be complete. What needs to be known about these families to predict their buying behavior? What does "lifestyle" include? How would we quantify some of these variables?

- A hypothesis was presented that catalog size and product diversity drive higher sales. What do we need to know to assess the validity of this hypothesis? Another hypothesis was presented about the quality of the translation. What was the evidence for this hypothesis? Is this a mathematical question? Sales may also be proportional to the amount of time a potential customer retains the catalog. How could one ascertain this?

- Despite the abundance of data, much uncertainty remains about what to expect from sales over the first two years. Analysis could be conducted with the data about the possible inventory consequences of choosing the wrong scenario.

- One might wonder about the uncertainty in size scales. What is so difficult about identifying the colors that Japanese people prefer? Can these preferences be predicted? Will this increase the complexity of the inventory management task?

- Can we predict how many people will not use phones? What do they use instead?

As seen through a mathematical lens, the business world can be a rich, complex, and essentially limitless source of fascinating questions.

NOTE
1. Return on investment.

ROL FESSENDEN is Vice-President of Inventory Planning and Control at L.L. Bean, Inc. He is also Co-Principal Investigator and Vice-Chair of Maine's State Systemic Initiative and Chair of the Strategic Planning Committee. He has previously served on the Mathematical Science Education Board, and on the National Alliance for State Science and Mathematics Coalitions (NASSMC).

3 INTEGRATING VOCATIONAL AND ACADEMIC EDUCATION

THOMAS BAILEY
COLUMBIA UNIVERSITY

In high school education, preparation for work immediately after high school and preparation for post-secondary education have traditionally been viewed as incompatible. Work-bound high-school students end up in vocational education tracks, where courses usually emphasize specific skills with little attention to underlying theoretical and conceptual foundations.[1] College-bound students proceed through traditional academic discipline-based courses, where they learn English, history, science, mathematics, and foreign languages, with only weak and often contrived references to applications of these skills in the workplace or in the community outside the school. To be sure, many vocational teachers do teach underlying concepts, and many academic teachers motivate their lessons with examples and references to the world outside the classroom. But these enrichments are mostly frills, not central to either the content or pedagogy of secondary school education.

RETHINKING VOCATIONAL AND ACADEMIC EDUCATION

Educational thinking in the United States has traditionally placed priority on college preparation. Thus the distinct track of vocational education has been seen as an option for those students who are deemed not capable of success in the more desirable academic track. As vocational programs acquired a reputation as a "dumping ground," a strong background in vocational courses (especially if they reduced credits in the core academic courses) has been viewed as a threat to the college aspirations of secondary school students.

This notion was further reinforced by the very influential 1983 report entitled *A Nation at Risk* (National Commission on Excellence in Education, 1983), which excoriated the U.S. educational system for moving away from an emphasis on core academic subjects that, according to the report, had been the basis of a previously successful American education system. Vocational courses were seen as diverting high school students from core academic activities. Despite the dubious empirical foundation of the report's conclusions, subsequent reforms in most states increased the number of academic courses required for graduation and reduced opportunities for students to take vocational courses.

The distinction between vocational students and college-bound students has always had a conceptual flaw. The large majority of students who go to four-year colleges are motivated, at least to a significant extent, by vocational objectives. In 1994, almost 247,000 bachelors degrees were conferred in business administration. That was only 30,000 less than the total number (277,500) of 1994 bachelor degrees conferred in English, mathematics, philosophy, religion, physical sciences and science technologies, biological and life sciences, social sciences, and history *combined*. Furthermore, these "academic" fields are also vocational since many students who graduate with these degrees intend to make their living working in those fields.

Several recent economic, technological, and educational trends challenge this sharp distinction between preparation for college and for immediate post-high-school work, or, more specifically, challenge the notion that students planning to work after high school have little need for academic skills while college-bound students are best served by an abstract education with only tenuous contact with the world of work:

1. First, many employers and analysts are arguing that, due to changes in the nature of work, traditional approaches to teaching vocational skills may not be effective in the future. Given the increasing pace of change and uncertainty in the workplace, young people will be better prepared, even for entry level positions and certainly for subsequent positions, if they have an underlying understanding of the scientific, mathematical, social, and even cultural aspects of the work that they will do. This has led to a growing emphasis on integrating academic and vocational education.[2]

2. Views about teaching and pedagogy have increasingly moved toward a more open and collaborative "student-centered" or "constructivist" teaching style that puts a great deal of emphasis on having students work together on complex, open-ended projects. This reform strategy is now widely implemented through the efforts of organizations such as the Coalition of Essential Schools, the National Center for Restructuring Education, Schools, and Teaching at

Teachers College, and the Center for Education Research at the University of Wisconsin at Madison. Advocates of this approach have not had much interaction with vocational educators and have certainly not advocated any emphasis on directly preparing high school students for work. Nevertheless, the approach fits well with a reformed education that integrates vocational and academic skills through authentic applications. Such applications offer opportunities to explore and combine mathematical, scientific, historical, literary, sociological, economic, and cultural issues.

3. In a related trend, the federal School-to-Work Opportunities Act of 1994 defines an educational strategy that combines constructivist pedagogical reforms with guided experiences in the workplace or other non-work settings. At its best, school-to-work could further integrate academic and vocational learning through appropriately designed experiences at work.

4. The integration of vocational and academic education and the initiatives funded by the School-to-Work Opportunities Act were originally seen as strategies for preparing students for work after high school or community college. Some educators and policy makers are becoming convinced that these approaches can also be effective for teaching academic skills and preparing students for four-year college. Teaching academic skills in the context of realistic and complex applications from the workplace and community can provide motivational benefits and may impart a deeper understanding of the material by showing students how the academic skills are actually used. Retention may also be enhanced by giving students a chance to apply the knowledge that they often learn only in the abstract.[3]

5. During the last twenty years, the real wages of high school graduates have fallen and the gap between the wages earned by high school and college graduates has grown significantly. Adults with no education beyond high school have very little chance of earning enough money to support a family with a moderate lifestyle.[4] Given these wage trends, it seems appropriate and just that every high school student at least be prepared for college, even if some choose to work immediately after high school.

INNOVATIVE EXAMPLES

There are many examples of programs that use work-related applications both to teach academic skills and to prepare students for college. One approach is to organize high school programs around broad industrial or occupational areas, such as health, agriculture, hospitality, manufacturing, transportation, or the arts. These broad areas offer many opportunities for wide-ranging curricula in all academic disciplines. They also offer opportunities for collaborative work among teachers from different disciplines. Specific skills can still be taught in this format but in such a way as to motivate broader academic and theoretical themes. Innovative programs can now be found in many vocational high schools in large cities, such as Aviation High School in New York City and the High School of Agricultural Science and Technology in Chicago. Other schools have organized schools-within-schools based on broad industry areas.

Agriculturally based activities, such as 4H and Future Farmers of America, have for many years used the farm setting and students' interest in farming to teach a variety of skills. It takes only a little imagination to think of how to use the social, economic, and scientific bases of agriculture to motivate and illustrate skills and knowledge from all of the academic disciplines. Many schools are now using internships and projects based on local business activities as teaching tools. One example among many is the integrated program offered by the Thomas Jefferson High School for Science and Technology in Virginia, linking biology, English, and technology through an environmental issues forum. Students work as partners with resource managers at the Mason Neck National Wildlife Refuge and the Mason Neck State Park to collect data and monitor the daily activities of various species that inhabit the region. They search current literature to establish a hypothesis related to a real world problem, design an experiment to test their hypothesis, run the experiment, collect and analyze data, draw conclusions, and produce a written document that communicates the results of the experiment. The students are even responsible for determining what information and resources are needed and how to access them. Student projects have included making plans for public education programs dealing with environmental matters, finding solutions to problems caused by encroaching land development, and making suggestions for how to handle the overabundance of deer in the region.

These examples suggest the potential that a more integrated education could have for all students. Thus continuing to maintain a sharp distinction between vocational and academic instruction in high school does not serve the interests of many of those students headed for four-year or two-year college or of those who expect to work after high school. Work-bound students will be better prepared for work if they have stronger academic skills, and a high quality curriculum that integrates school-based learning into work and community applications is an effective way to teach academic skills for many students.

Despite the many examples of innovative initiatives that suggest the potential for an integrated view, the legacy of the duality between vocational and academic education and the low status of work-related studies in high school continue to influence education and education reform. In general, programs that deviate from traditional college-prep organization and format are still viewed with suspicion by parents and teachers focused on four-year college. Indeed, college admissions practices still very much favor the traditional approaches. Interdisciplinary courses, "applied" courses, internships, and other types of work experience that characterize the school-to-work strategy or programs that integrate academic and vocational education often do not fit well into college admissions requirements.

Joining Work and Learning

What implications does this have for the mathematics standards developed by the National Council of Teachers of Mathematics (NCTM)? The general principle should be to try to design standards that challenge rather than reinforce the distinction between vocational and academic instruction. Academic teachers of mathematics and those working to set academic standards need to continue to try to understand the use of mathematics in the workplace and in everyday life. Such understandings would offer insights that could suggest reform of the traditional curriculum, but they would also provide a better foundation for teaching mathematics using realistic applications. The examples in this volume are particularly instructive because they suggest the importance of problem solving, logic, and imagination and show that these are all important parts of mathematical applications in realistic work settings. But these are only a beginning.

In order to develop this approach, it would be helpful if the NCTM standards writers worked closely with groups that are setting industry standards[5]. This would allow both groups to develop a deeper understanding of the mathematics content of work.

The NCTM's Curriculum Standards for Grades 9-12 include both core standards for all students and additional standards for "college-intending" students. The argument presented in this essay suggests that the NCTM should dispense with the distinction between college intending and non-college intending students. Most of the additional standards, those intended only for the "college intending" students, provide background that is necessary or beneficial for the calculus sequence. A re-evaluation of the role of calculus in the high school curriculum may be appropriate, but calculus should not serve as a wedge to separate college-bound from non-college-bound students. Clearly, some high school students will take calculus, although many college-bound students will not take calculus either in high school or in college. Thus in practice, calculus is not a characteristic that distinguishes between those who are or are not headed for college. Perhaps standards for a variety of options beyond the core might be offered. Mathematics standards should be set to encourage stronger skills for all students and to illustrate the power and usefulness of mathematics in many settings. They should not be used to institutionalize dubious distinctions between groups of students.

References

Bailey, T. & Merritt, D. (1997). *School-to-work for the college bound.* Berkeley, CA: National Center for Research in Vocational Education.

Hoachlander, G. (1997). Organizing mathematics education around work. In L.A. Steen (Ed.), *Why numbers count: Quantitative literacy for tomorrow's America*, (pp. 122-136). New York: College Entrance Examination Board.

Levy, F. & Murnane, R. (1992). U.S. earnings levels and earnings inequality: A review of recent trends and proposed explanations. *Journal of Economic Literature, 30*, 1333-1381.

National Commission on Excellence in Education. (1983). *A nation at risk: The imperative for educational reform.* Washington, DC: Author.

NOTES

1. Vocational education has been shaped by federal legislation since the first vocational education act was passed in 1917. According to the current legislation, the Carl D. Perkins Vocational and Technical Education Act of 1990, vocational students are those not headed for a baccalaureate degree, so they include both students expecting to work immediately after high school as well as those expecting to go to a community college.

2. This point of view underlies the reforms articulated in the 1990 reauthorization of the Carl Perkins Vocational and Technical Education Act (VATEA). VATEA also promoted a program, dubbed "tech-prep," that established formal articulations between secondary school and community college curricula.

3. This argument is reviewed in Bailey & Merritt (1997). For an argument about how education may be organized around broad work themes can enhance learning in mathematics see Hoachlander (1997).

4. These wage data are reviewed in Levy & Murnane (1992).

5. The Goals 2000: Educate America Act, for example, established the National Skill Standards Board in 1994 to serve as a catalyst in the development of a voluntary national system of skills standards, assessments, and certifications for business and industry.

THOMAS BAILEY is an Associate Professor of Economics Education at Teachers College, Columbia University. He is also Director of the Institute on Education and the Economy and Director of the Community College Research Center, both at Teachers College. He is also on the board of the National Center for Research in Vocational Education.

4 The Importance of Workplace and Everyday Mathematics

Jean E. Taylor
Rutgers University

For decades our industrial society has been based on fossil fuels. In today's knowledge-based society, mathematics is the energy that drives the system. In the words of the new WQED television series, *Life by the Numbers*, to create knowledge we "burn mathematics." Mathematics is more than a fixed tool applied in known ways. New mathematical techniques and analyses and even conceptual frameworks are continually required in economics, in finance, in materials science, in physics, in biology, in medicine.

Just as all scientific and health-service careers are mathematically based, so are many others. Interaction with computers has become a part of more and more jobs, and good analytical skills enhance computer use and troubleshooting. In addition, virtually all levels of management and many support positions in business and industry require some mathematical understanding, including an ability to read graphs and interpret other information presented visually, to use estimation effectively, and to apply mathematical reasoning.

What Should Students Learn for Today's World?

Education in mathematics and the ability to communicate its predictions is more important than ever for moving from low-paying jobs into better-paying ones. For example, my local paper, *The Times of Trenton*, had a section "Focus on Careers" on October 5, 1997 in which the majority of the ads were for high technology careers (many more than for sales and marketing, for example).

But precisely what mathematics should students learn in school? Mathematicians and mathematics educators have been discussing this question for decades. This essay presents some thoughts about three areas of mathematics—estimation, trigonometry, and algebra—and then some thoughts about teaching and learning.

Estimation is one of the harder skills for students to learn, even if they experience relatively little difficulty with other aspects of mathematics. Many students think of mathematics as a set of precise rules yielding exact answers and are uncomfortable with the idea of imprecise answers, especially when the degree of precision in the estimate depends on the context and is not itself given by a rule. Yet it is very important to be able to get an approximate sense of the size an answer should be, as a way to get a rough check on the accuracy of a calculation (I've personally used it in stores to detect that I've been charged twice for the same item, as well as often in my own mathematical work), a feasibility estimate, or as an estimation for tips.

Trigonometry plays a significant role in the sciences and can help us understand phenomena in everyday life. Often introduced as a study of triangle measurement, trigonometry may be used for surveying and for determining heights of trees, but its utility extends vastly beyond these triangular applications. Students can experience the power of mathematics by using sine and cosine to model periodic phenomena such as going around and around a circle, going in and out with tides, monitoring temperature or smog components changing on a 24-hour cycle, or the cycling of predator-prey populations.

No educator argues the importance of algebra for students aiming for mathematically-based careers because of the foundation it provides for the more specialized education they will need later. Yet, algebra is also important for those students who do not currently aspire to mathematics-based careers, in part because a lack of algebraic skills puts an upper bound on the types of careers to which a student can aspire. Former civil rights leader Robert Moses makes a good case for every student learning algebra, as a means of empowering students and providing goals, skills, and opportunities. The same idea was applied to learning calculus in the movie *Stand and Deliver*. How, then, can we help all students learn algebra?

For me personally, the impetus to learn algebra was at least in part to learn methods of solution for puzzles. Suppose you have 39 jars on three shelves. There are twice as many jars on the second shelf as the first, and four more jars on the third shelf than on the second shelf. How many jars are there on each shelf? Such problems are not important by themselves, but if they show the students the power of an idea by enabling them to solve puzzles that they'd like to solve, then they have value. We can't expect such problems to interest all students. How then can we reach more students?

WORKPLACE AND EVERYDAY SETTINGS AS A WAY OF MAKING SENSE

One of the common tools in business and industry for investigating mathematical issues is the spreadsheet, which is closely related to algebra. Writing a rule to combine the elements of certain cells to produce the quantity that goes into another cell is doing algebra, although the variables names are cell names rather than x or y. Therefore, setting up spreadsheet analyses requires some of the thinking that algebra requires.

By exploring mathematics via tasks which come from workplace and everyday settings, and with the aid of common tools like spreadsheets, students are more likely to see the relevance of the mathematics and are more likely to learn it in ways that are personally meaningful than when it is presented abstractly and applied later only if time permits. Thus, this essay argues that workplace and everyday tasks should be used for teaching mathematics and, in particular, for teaching algebra. It would be a mistake, however, to rely exclusively on such tasks, just as it would be a mistake to teach only spreadsheets in place of algebra.

Communicating the results of an analysis is a fundamental part of any use of mathematics on a job. There is a growing emphasis in the workplace on group work and on the skills of communicating ideas to colleagues and clients. But communicating mathematical ideas is also a powerful tool for learning, for it requires the student to sharpen often fuzzy ideas.

Some of the tasks in this volume can provide the kinds of opportunities I am talking about. Another problem, with clear connections to the real world, is the following, taken from the book entitled *Consider a Spherical Cow: A Course in Environmental Problem Solving*, by John Harte (1988). The question posed is: How does biomagnification of a trace substance occur? For example, how do pesticides accumulate in the food chain, becoming concentrated in predators such as condors? Specifically, identify the critical ecological and chemical parameters determining bioconcentrations in a food chain, and in terms of these parameters, derive a formula for the concentration of a trace substance in each link of a food chain. This task can be undertaken at several different levels. The analysis in Harte's book is at a fairly high level, although it still involves only algebra as a mathematical tool. The task could be undertaken at a more simple level or, on the other hand, it could be elaborated upon as suggested by further exercises given in that book. And the students could then present the results of their analyses to each other as well as the teacher, in oral or written form.

CONCEPTS OR PROCEDURES?

When teaching mathematics, it is easy to spend so much time and energy focusing on the procedures that the concepts receive little if any attention. When teaching algebra, students often learn the procedures for using the quadratic formula or for solving simultaneous equations without thinking of intersections of curves and lines and without being able to apply the procedures in unfamiliar settings. Even when concentrating on word problems, students often learn the procedures for solving "coin problems" and "train problems" but don't see the larger algebraic context. The formulas and procedures are important, but are not enough.

When using workplace and everyday tasks for teaching mathematics, we must avoid falling into the same trap of focusing on the procedures at the expense of the concepts. Avoiding the trap is not easy, however, because just like many tasks in school algebra, mathematically based workplace tasks often have standard procedures that can be used without an understanding of the underlying mathematics. To change a procedure to accommodate a changing business climate, to respond to changes in the tax laws, or to apply or modify a procedure to accommodate a similar situation, however, requires an understanding of the mathematical ideas behind the procedures. In particular, a student should be able to modify the procedures for assessing energy usage for heating (as in **Heating-Degree-Days,** p. 54) in order to assess energy usage for cooling in the summer.

To prepare our students to make such modifications on their own, it is important to focus on the concepts as well as the procedures. Workplace and everyday tasks can provide opportunities for students to attach meaning to the mathematical calculations and procedures. If a student initially solves a problem without algebra, then the thinking that went into his or her solution can help him or her make sense out of algebraic approaches that are later presented by the teacher or by other students. Such an approach is especially appropriate for teaching algebra, because our teaching of algebra needs to reach more students (too often it is seen by students as meaningless symbol manipulation) and because algebraic thinking is increasingly important in the workplace.

AN EXAMPLE: THE STUDENT/PROFESSOR PROBLEM

To illustrate the complexity of learning algebra meaningfully, consider the following problem from a study by Clement, Lockhead, & Monk (1981):

> Write an equation for the following statement: "There are six times as many students as professors at this university." Use S for the number of students and P for the number of professors. (p. 288)

The authors found that of 47 nonscience majors taking college algebra, 57% got it wrong. What is more surprising, however, is that of 150 calculus-level students, 37% missed the problem.

A first reaction to the most common wrong answer, $6S = P$, is that the students simply translated the words of the problems into mathematical symbols without thinking more deeply about the situation or the variables. (The authors note that some textbooks instruct students to use such translation.)

By analyzing transcripts of interviews with students, the authors found this approach and another (faulty) approach, as well. These students often drew a diagram showing six students and one professor. (Note that we often instruct students to draw diagrams when solving word problems.) Reasoning from the diagram, and regarding S and P as units, the student may write $6S = P$, just as we would correctly write 12 in. = 1 ft. Such reasoning is quite sensible, though it misses the fundamental intent in the problem statement that S is to represent the number of students, not a student.

Thus, two common suggestions for students—word-for-word translation and drawing a diagram—can lead to an incorrect answer to this apparently simple problem, if the students do not more deeply contemplate what the variables are intended to represent. The authors found that students who wrote and could explain the correct answer, $S = 6P$, drew upon a richer understanding of what the equation and the variables represent.

Clearly, then, we must encourage students to contemplate the meanings of variables. Yet, part of the power and efficiency of algebra is precisely that one can manipulate symbols independently of what they mean and then draw meaning out of the conclusions to which the symbolic manipulations lead. Thus, stable, long-term learning of algebraic thinking requires both mastery of procedures and also deeper analytical thinking.

CONCLUSION

Paradoxically, the need for sharper analytical thinking occurs alongside a decreased need for routine arithmetic calculation. Calculators and computers make routine calculation easier to do quickly and accurately; cash registers used in fast food restaurants sometimes return change; checkout counters have bar code readers and payment takes place by credit cards or money-access cards.

So it is education in mathematical thinking, in applying mathematical computation, in assessing whether an answer is reasonable, and in communicating the results that is essential. Teaching mathematics via workplace and everyday problems is an approach that can make mathematics more meaningful for all students. It is important, however, to go beyond the specific details of a task in order to teach mathematical ideas. While this approach is particularly crucial for those students intending to pursue careers in the mathematical sciences, it will also lead to deeper mathematical understanding for all students.

REFERENCES

Clement, J., Lockhead, J., & Monk, G. (1981). Translation difficulties in learning mathematics. *American Mathematical Monthly, 88,* 286-290.

Harte, J. (1988). *Consider a spherical cow : A course in environmental problem solving.* York, PA: University Science Books.

JEAN E. TAYLOR is Professor of Mathematics at Rutgers, the State University of New Jersey. She is currently a member of the Board of Directors of the American Association for the Advancement of Science and formerly chaired its Section A Nominating Committee. She has served as Vice President and as a Member-at-Large of the Council of the American Mathematical Society, and served on its Executive Committee and its Nominating Committee. She has also been a member of the Joint Policy Board for Mathematics, and a member of the Board of Advisors to The Geometry Forum (now The Mathematics Forum) and to the WQED television series, *Life by the Numbers.*

5

WORKING WITH ALGEBRA

DANIEL CHAZAN
MICHIGAN STATE UNIVERSITY

SANDRA CALLIS BETHELL
HOLT HIGH SCHOOL

Teaching a mathematics class in which few of the students have demonstrated success is a difficult assignment. Many teachers avoid such assignments, when possible. On the one hand, high school mathematics teachers, like Bertrand Russell, might love mathematics and believe something like the following:

> Mathematics, rightly viewed, possesses not only truth, but supreme beauty—a beauty cold and austere, like that of sculpture, without appeal to any part of our weaker nature, without the gorgeous trappings of painting or music, yet sublimely pure, and capable of a stern perfection such as only the greatest art can show. . . . Remote from human passions, remote even from the pitiful facts of nature, the generations have gradually created an ordered cosmos, where pure thought can dwell as in its nature home, and where one, at least, of our nobler impulses can escape from the dreary exile of the natural world. (Russell, 1910, p. 73)

But, on the other hand, students may not have the luxury, in their circumstances, of appreciating this beauty. Many of them may not see themselves as thinkers because contemplation would take them away from their primary focus: how to get by in a world that was not created for them. Instead, like Jamaica Kincaid, they may be asking:

> What makes the world turn against me and all who look like me? I won nothing, I survey nothing, when I ask this question, the luxury of an answer that will fill volumes does not stretch out before me. When I ask this question, my voice is filled with despair. (Kincaid, 1996, pp. 131-132)

OUR TEACHING AND ISSUES IT RAISED

During the 1991-92 and 1992-93 school years, we (a high school teacher and a university teacher educator) team taught a lower track Algebra I class for 10th through 12th grade students.[1] Most of our students had failed mathematics before, and many needed to pass Algebra I in order to complete their high school mathematics requirement for graduation. For our students, mathematics had become a charged subject; it carried a heavy burden of negative experiences. Many of our students were convinced that neither they nor their peers could be successful in mathematics.

Few of our students did well in other academic subjects, and few were headed on to two- or four-year colleges. But the students differed in their affiliation with the high school. Some, called "preppies" or "jocks" by others, were active participants in the school's activities. Others, "smokers" or "stoners," were rebelling to differing degrees against school and more broadly against society. There were strong tensions between members of these groups.[2]

Teaching in this setting gives added importance and urgency to the typical questions of curriculum and motivation common to most algebra classes. In our teaching, we explored questions such as the following:

- What is it that we really want high school students, especially those who are not college-intending, to study in algebra and why?

- What is the role of algebra's manipulative skills in a world with graphing calculators and computers? How do the manipulative skills taught in the traditional curriculum give students a new perspective on, and insight into, our world?

- If our teaching efforts depend on students' investment in learning, on what grounds can we appeal to them, implicitly or explicitly, for energy and effort? In a tracked, compulsory setting, how can we help students, with broad interests and talents and many of whom are not college-intending, see value in a shared exploration of algebra?

AN APPROACH TO SCHOOL ALGEBRA

As a result of thinking about these questions, in our teaching we wanted to avoid being in the position of exhorting students to appreciate the beauty or utility of algebra. Our students were frankly skeptical of arguments based on utility. They saw few people in their community using algebra. We had also lost faith in the power of extrinsic rewards and punishments, like failing grades. Many of our students were skeptical of the power of the high school diploma to alter fundamentally their life circumstances. We wanted students to find the mathematical objects we were discussing in the world around them and thus learn to value the perspective that this mathematics might give them on their world.

To help us in this task, we found it useful to take what we call a "relationships between quantities" approach to school algebra. In this approach, the fundamental mathematical objects of study in school algebra are functions that can be represented by inputs and outputs listed in tables or sketched or plotted on graphs, as well as calculation procedures that can be written with algebraic symbols.[3] Stimulated, in part, by the following quote from August Comte, we viewed these functions as mathematical representations of theories people have developed for explaining relationships between quantities.

> In the light of previous experience, we must acknowledge the impossibility of determining, by direct measurement, most of the heights and distances we should like to know. It is this general fact which makes the science of mathematics necessary. For in renouncing the hope, in almost every case, of measuring great heights or distances directly, the human mind has had to attempt to determine them indirectly, and it is thus that philosophers were led to invent mathematics. (Quoted in Serres, 1982, p. 85)

THE "SPONSOR" PROJECT

Using this approach to the concept of function, during the 1992-93 school year, we designed a year-long project for our students. The project asked pairs of students to find the mathematical objects we were studying in the workplace of a community sponsor. Students visited the sponsor's workplace four times during the year—three after-school visits and one day-long excused absence from school. In these visits, the students came to know the workplace and learned about the sponsor's work. We then asked students to write a report describing the sponsor's workplace and answering questions about the nature of the mathematical activity embedded in the workplace. The questions are organized in Table 5-1.

USING THESE QUESTIONS

In order to determine how the interviews could be structured and to provide students with a model, we chose to interview Sandra's husband, John Bethell, who is a coatings inspector for an engineering firm. When asked about his job, John responded, "I argue for a living." He went on to describe his daily work inspecting contractors painting water towers. Since most municipalities contract with the lowest bidder when a water tower needs to be painted, they will often hire an engineering firm to make sure that the contractor works according to specification. Since the contractor has made a low bid, there are strong

TABLE 5-1: Questions to ask in the workplace
QUANTITIES: MEASURED OR COUNTED VERSUS COMPUTED
• What quantities are measured or counted by the people you interview?
• What kinds of tools are used to measure or count?
• Why is it important to measure or count these quantities?
• What quantities do they compute or calculate?
• What kinds of tools are used to do the computing?
• Why is it important to compute these quantities?
COMPUTING QUANTITIES
• When a quantity is computed, what information is needed and then what computations are done to get the desired result?
• Are there ever different ways to compute the same thing?
REPRESENTING QUANTITIES AND RELATIONSHIPS BETWEEN QUANTITIES
• How are quantities kept track of or represented in this line of work?
• Collect examples of graphs, charts, tables, etc. that are used in the business.
• How is information presented to clients or to others who work in the business?
COMPARISONS
• What kinds of comparisons are made with computed quantities?
• Why are these comparisons important to do?
• What set of actions are set into motion as a result of interpretation of the computations?

financial incentives for the contractor to compromise on quality in order to make a profit.

In his work John does different kinds of inspections. For example, he has a magnetic instrument to check the thickness of the paint once it has been applied to the tower. When it gives a "thin" reading, contractors often question the technology. To argue for the reading, John uses the surface area of the tank, the number of paint cans used, the volume of paint in the can, and an understanding of the percentage of this volume that evaporates to calculate the average thickness of the dry coating. Other examples from his workplace involve the use of tables and measuring instruments of different kinds.

SOME EXAMPLES OF STUDENTS' WORK

When school started, students began working on their projects. Although many of the sponsors initially indicated that there were no mathematical dimensions to their work, students often were able to show sponsors places where the mathematics we were studying was to be found. For example, Jackie worked with a crop and soil scientist. She was intrigued by the way in which measurement of weight is used to count seeds. First, her sponsor would weigh a test batch of 100 seeds to generate a benchmark weight. Then, instead of counting a large number of seeds, the scientist would weigh an amount of seeds and compute the number of seeds such a weight would contain.

Rebecca worked with a carpeting contractor who, in estimating costs, read the dimensions of rectangular rooms off an architect's blueprint, multiplied to find the area of the room in square feet (doing conversions where necessary), then multiplied by a cost per square foot (which depended on the type of carpet) to compute the cost of the carpet. The purpose of these estimates was to prepare a bid for the architect where the bid had to be as low as possible without making the job unprofitable. Rebecca used a chart (Table 5-2) to explain this procedure to the class.

Joe and Mick, also working in construction, found out that in laying pipes, there is a "one by one" rule of thumb. When digging a trench for the placement of the pipe, the non-parallel sides of the trapezoidal cross section must have a slope of 1 foot down for every one foot across. This ratio guarantees that the dirt in the hole will not slide down on itself. Thus, if at the bottom of the hole, the trapezoid must have a certain width in order to fit the pipe, then on ground level the hole must be this width plus twice the depth of the hole. Knowing in advance how wide the hole must be avoids lengthy and costly trial and error.

Other students found that functions were often embedded in cultural artifacts found in the workplace. For example, a student who visited a doctor's office brought in an instrument for predicting the due dates of pregnant women, as well as providing information about average fetal weight and length (Figure 5-1).

TABLE 5-2: Cost of carpet worksheet			
INPUTS			OUTPUT
LENGTH	WIDTH	AREA OF THE ROOM	COST FOR CARPETING ROOM
10	35		
20	25		
15	30		

FIGURE 5-1: Pregnancy wheel

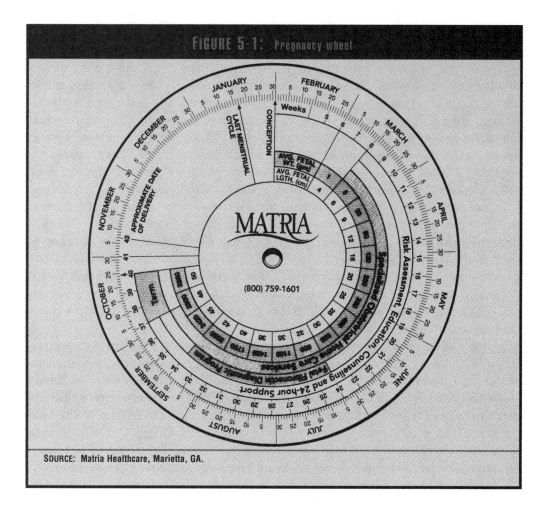

SOURCE: Matria Healthcare, Marietta, GA.

CONCLUSION

While the complexities of organizing this sort of project should not be mini-mized—arranging sponsors, securing parental permission, and meeting admin-istrators and parent concerns about the requirement of off-campus, after-school work—we remain intrigued by the potential of such projects for helping students see mathematics in the world around them. The notions of identify-ing central mathematical objects for a course and then developing ways of iden-tifying those objects in students' experience seems like an important alterna-tive to the use of application-based materials written by developers whose lives and social worlds may be quite different from those of students.

REFERENCES

Chazen, D. (1996). Algebra for all students? *Journal of Mathematical Behavior, 15*(4), 455-477.
Eckert, P. (1989). *Jocks and burnouts: Social categories and identity in the high school.* New York: Teachers College Press.

Fey, J. T., Heid, M. K., et al. (1995). *Concepts in algebra: A technological approach*. Dedham, MA: Janson Publications.

Kieran, C., Boileau, A., & Garancon, M. (1996). Introducing algebra by means of a technology-supported, functional approach. In N. Bednarz et al. (Eds.), *Approaches to algebra*, (pp. 257-293). Kluwer Academic Publishers: Dordrecht, The Netherlands.

Kincaid, J. (1996). *The autobiography of my mother*. New York: Farrar, Straus, Giroux.

Nemirovsky, R. (1996). Mathematical narratives, modeling and algebra. In N. Bednarz et al. (Eds.) *Approaches to algebra*, (pp. 197-220). Kluwer Academic Publishers: Dordrecht, The Netherlands.

Russell, B. (1910). *Philosophical Essays*. London: Longmans, Green.

Schwartz, J. & Yerushalmy, M. (1992). Getting students to function in and with algebra. In G. Harel & E. Dubinsky (Eds.), *The concept of function: Aspects of epistemology and pedagogy*, (MAA Notes, Vol. 25, pp. 261-289). Washington, DC: Mathematical Association of America.

Serres, M. (1982). Mathematics and philosophy: What Thales saw . . . In J. Harari & D. Bell (Eds.), *Hermes: Literature, science, philosophy*, (pp. 84-97). Baltimore, MD: Johns Hopkins.

Thompson, P. (1993). Quantitative reasoning, complexity, and additive structures. *Educational Studies in Mathematics*, *25*, 165-208.

Yerushalmy, M. & Schwartz, J. L. (1993). Seizing the opportunity to make algebra mathematically and pedagogically interesting. In T. A. Romberg, E. Fennema, & T. P. Carpenter (Eds.), *Integrating research on the graphical representation of functions*, (pp. 41-68). Hillsdale, NJ: Lawrence Erlbaum Associates.

NOTES

1. For other details, see Chazan (1996).
2. For more detail on high school students' social groups, see Eckert (1989).
3. Our ideas have been greatly influenced by Schwartz & Yerushalmy (1992) and Yerushalmy & Schwartz (1993) and are in the same spirit as the approach taken by Fey, Heid, et al. (1995), Kieran, Boileau, & Garancon (1996), Nemirovsky (1996), and Thompson (1993).

DANIEL CHAZAN is an Associate Professor of Teacher Education at Michigan State University. To assist his research in mathematics teaching and learning, he has taught algebra at the high school level. His interests include teaching mathematics by examining student ideas, using computers to support student exploration, and the potential for the history and philosophy of mathematics to inform teaching.

SANDRA CALLIS BETHELL has taught mathematics and Spanish at Holt High School for 10 years. She has also completed graduate work at Michigan State University and Western Michigan University. She has interest in mathematics reform, particularly in meeting the needs of diverse learners in algebra courses.

EMERGENCY CALLS

TASK. A city is served by two different ambulance companies. City logs record the date, the time of the call, the ambulance company, and the response time for each 911 call (Table 1). Analyze these data and write a report to the City Council (with supporting charts and graphs) advising it on which ambulance company the 911 operators should choose to dispatch for calls from this region.

DATE OF CALL	TIME OF CALL	COMPANY NAME	RESPONSE TIME IN MINUTES	DATE OF CALL	TIME OF CALL	COMPANY NAME	RESPONSE TIME IN MINUTES
\multicolumn{8}{c}{**TABLE 1:** Ambulance dispatch log sheet, May 1–30}
1	7:12 AM	Metro	11	12	8:30 PM	Arrow	8
1	7:43 PM	Metro	11	15	1:03 AM	Metro	12
2	10:02 PM	Arrow	7	15	6:40 AM	Arrow	17
2	12:22 PM	Metro	12	15	3:25 PM	Metro	15
3	5:30 AM	Arrow	17	16	4:15 AM	Metro	7
3	6:18 PM	Arrow	6	16	8:41 AM	Arrow	19
4	6:25 AM	Arrow	16	18	2:39 PM	Arrow	10
5	8:56 PM	Metro	10	18	3:44 PM	Metro	14
6	4:59 PM	Metro	14	19	6:33 AM	Metro	6
7	2:20 AM	Arrow	11	22	7:25 AM	Arrow	17
7	12:41 PM	Arrow	8	22	4:20 PM	Metro	19
7	2:29 PM	Metro	11	24	4:21 PM	Arrow	9
8	8:14 AM	Metro	8	25	8:07 AM	Arrow	15
8	6:23 PM	Metro	16	25	5:02 PM	Arrow	7
9	6:47 AM	Metro	9	26	10:51 AM	Metro	9
9	7:15 AM	Arrow	16	26	5:11 PM	Metro	18
9	6:10 PM	Arrow	8	27	4:16 AM	Arrow	10
10	5:37 PM	Metro	16	29	8:59 AM	Metro	11
10	9:37 PM	Metro	11	30	11:09 AM	Arrow	7
11	10:11 AM	Metro	8	30	9:15 PM	Arrow	8
11	11:45 AM	Metro	10	30	11:15 PM	Metro	8

COMMENTARY. This problem confronts the student with a realistic situation and a body of data regarding two ambulance companies' response times to emergency calls. The data the student is provided are typically "messy"—just a log of calls and response times, ordered chronologically. The question is how to make sense of them. Finding patterns in data such as these requires a productive mixture of mathematics, common sense, and intellectual detective work. It's the kind of reasoning that students should be able to do—the kind of reasoning that will pay off in the real world.

MATHEMATICAL ANALYSIS. In this case, a numerical analysis is not especially informative. On average, the companies are about the same: Arrow has a mean response time of 11.4 minutes compared to 11.6 minutes for Metro. The spread of the data is also not very helpful. The ranges of their distributions are exactly the same: from 6 minutes to 19 minutes. The standard deviation of Arrow's response time is a little longer—4.3 minutes versus 3.4 minutes for Metro—indicating that Arrow's response times fluctuate a bit more.

Graphs of the response times (Figures 1 and 2) reveal interesting features. Both companies, especially Arrow, seem to have bimodal distributions, which is to say that there are two clusters of data without much data in between.

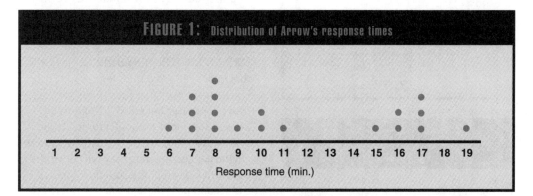

FIGURE 1: Distribution of Arrow's response times

Response time (min.)

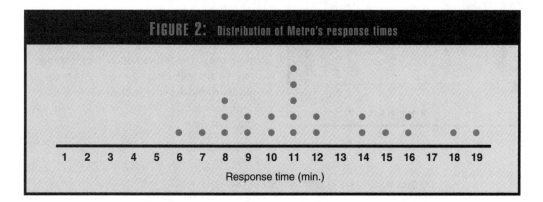

FIGURE 2: Distribution of Metro's response times

Response time (min.)

The distributions for both companies suggest that there are some other factors at work. Might a particular driver be the problem? Might the slow response times for either company be on particular days of the week or at particular times of day? Graphs of the response time versus the time of day (Figures 3 and 4) shed some light on these questions.

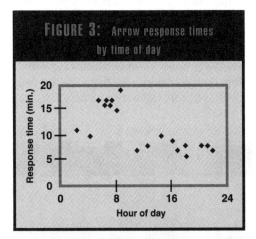

FIGURE 3: Arrow response times by time of day

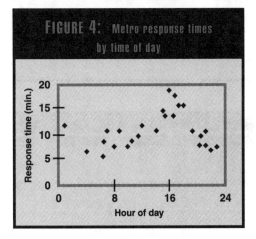

FIGURE 4: Metro response times by time of day

These graphs show that Arrow's response times were fast except between 5:30 AM and 9:00 AM, when they were about 9 minutes slower on average. Similarly, Metro's response times were fast except between about 3:30 PM and 6:30 PM, when they were about 5 minutes slower. Perhaps the locations of the companies make Arrow more susceptible to the morning rush hour and Metro more susceptible to the afternoon rush hour. On the other hand, the employees on Arrow's morning shift or Metro's afternoon shift may not be efficient. To avoid slow responses, one could recommend to the City Council that Metro be called during the morning and that Arrow be called during the afternoon. A little detective work into the sources of the differences between the companies may yield a better recommendation.

EXTENSIONS. Comparisons may be drawn between two samples in various contexts—response times for various services (taxis, computer-help desks, 24-hour hot lines at automobile manufacturers) being one class among many. Depending upon the circumstances, the data may tell very different stories. Even in the situation above, if the second pair of graphs hadn't offered such clear explanations, one might have argued that although the response times for Arrow were better on average the spread was larger, thus making their "extremes" more risky. The fundamental idea is using various analysis and representation techniques to make sense of data when the important factors are not necessarily known ahead of time.

BACK-OF-THE-ENVELOPE ESTIMATES

TASK. Practice "back-of-the-envelope" estimates based on rough approximations that can be derived from common sense or everyday observations. Examples:

- Consider a public high school mathematics teacher who feels that students should work five nights a week, averaging about 35 minutes a night, doing focused on-task work and who intends to grade all homework with comments and corrections. What is a reasonable number of hours per week that such a teacher should allocate for grading homework?

- How much paper does *The New York Times* use in a week? A paper company that wishes to make a bid to become their sole supplier needs to know whether they have enough current capacity. If the company were to store a two-week supply of newspaper, will their empty 14,000 square foot warehouse be big enough?

COMMENTARY. Some 50 years ago, physicist Enrico Fermi asked his students at the University of Chicago, "How many piano tuners are there in Chicago?" By asking such questions, Fermi wanted his students to make estimates that involved rough approximations so that their goal would be not precision but the order of magnitude of their result. Thus, many people today call these kinds of questions "Fermi questions." These generally rough calculations often require little more than common sense, everyday observations, and a scrap of paper, such as the back of a used envelope.

Scientists and mathematicians use the idea of *order of magnitude*, usually expressed as the closest power of ten, to give a rough sense of the size of a quantity. In everyday conversation, people use a similar idea when

they talk about "being in the right ballpark." For example, a full-time job at minimum wage yields an annual income on the order of magnitude of $10,000 or 10^4 dollars. Some corporate executives and professional athletes make annual salaries on the order of magnitude of $10,000,000 or 10^7 dollars. To say that these salaries differ by a factor of 1000 or 10^3, one can say that they differ by three orders of magnitude. Such a lack of precision might seem unscientific or unmathematical, but such approximations are quite useful in determining whether a more precise measurement is feasible or necessary, what sort of action might be required, or whether the result of a calculation is "in the right ballpark." In choosing a strategy to protect an endangered species, for example, scientists plan differently if there are 500 animals remaining than if there are 5,000. On the other hand, determining whether 5,200 or 6,300 is a better estimate is not necessary, as the strategies will probably be the same.

Careful reasoning with everyday observations can usually produce Fermi estimates that are within an order of magnitude of the exact answer (if there is one). Fermi estimates encourage students to reason creatively with approximate quantities and uncertain information. Experiences with such a process can help an individual function in daily life to determine the reasonableness of numerical calculations, of situations or ideas in the workplace, or of a proposed tax cut. A quick estimate of some revenue- or profit-enhancing scheme may show that the idea is comparable to suggesting that General Motors enter the summer sidewalk lemonade market in your neighborhood. A quick estimate could encourage further investigation or provide the rationale to dismiss the idea.

BACK-OF-THE-ENVELOPE (CONTINUED)

Almost any numerical claim may be treated as a Fermi question when the problem solver does not have access to all necessary background information. In such a situation, one may make rough guesses about relevant numbers, do a few calculations, and then produce estimates.

MATHEMATICAL ANALYSIS. The examples are solved separately below.

Grading Homework. Although many component factors vary greatly from teacher to teacher or even from week to week, rough calculations are not hard to make. Some important factors to consider for the teacher are: how many classes he or she teaches, how many students are in each of the classes, how much experience has the teacher had in general and has the teacher previously taught the classes, and certainly, as part of teaching style, the kind of homework the teacher assigns, not to mention the teacher's efficiency in grading.

Suppose the teacher has 5 classes averaging 25 students per class. Because the teacher plans to write corrections and comments, assume that the students' papers contain more than a list of answers—they show some student work and, perhaps, explain some of the solutions. Grading such papers might take as long as 10 minutes each, or perhaps even longer. Assuming that the teacher can grade them as quickly as 3 minutes each, on average, the teacher's grading time is:

$$3 \frac{\text{minutes}}{\text{student}} \times 25 \frac{\text{student}}{\text{class}} \times 5 \frac{\text{classes}}{\text{day}} \times 5 \frac{\text{days}}{\text{week}} =$$

$$1875 \frac{\text{minutes}}{\text{week}} \div 60 \frac{\text{minutes}}{\text{hour}} \approx 31 \frac{\text{hours}}{\text{week}}.$$

This is an impressively large number, especially for a teacher who already spends almost 25 hours/week in class, some additional time in preparation, and some time meeting with individual students. Is it reasonable to expect teachers to put in that kind of time? What compromises or other changes might the teacher make to reduce the amount of time? The calculation above offers four possibilities: Reduce the time spent on each homework paper, reduce the number of students per class, reduce the number of classes taught each day, or reduce the number of days per week that homework will be collected. If the teacher decides to spend at most 2 hours grading each night, what is the total number of students for which the teacher should have responsibility? This calculation is a partial reverse of the one above:

$$2 \frac{\text{hours}}{\text{day}} \times 60 \frac{\text{minutes}}{\text{hour}} \div 3 \frac{\text{minutes}}{\text{student}} = 40 \frac{\text{students}}{\text{day}}.$$

If the teacher still has 5 classes, that would mean 8 students per class!

The New York Times. Answering this question requires two preliminary estimates: the circulation of *The New York Times* and the size of the newspaper. The answers will probably be different on Sundays. Though *The New York Times* is a national newspaper, the number of subscribers outside the New York metropolitan area is probably small compared to the number inside. The population of the New York metropolitan area is roughly ten million people. Since most families buy at most one copy, and not all families buy *The New York Times*, the circulation might be about 1 million newspapers each day. (A circulation of 500,000 seems too small and 2 million seems too big.) The Sunday and weekday editions probably have different circulations, but assume that they are the same since they probably differ by less than a factor of two—much less than an order of magnitude. When folded, a weekday edition of the paper measures about 1/2 inch thick, a little more than 1 foot long, and about 1 foot wide. A Sunday edition of the paper is the same width and length, but perhaps 2 inches thick. For a week, then, the papers would stack $6 \times \frac{1}{2} + 2 = 5$ inches thick, for a total volume of about 1 ft $\times$ 1 ft $\times \frac{5}{12}$ ft ≈ 0.5 ft^3.

The whole circulation, then, would require about 1/2 million cubic feet of paper per week, or about 1 million cubic feet for a two-week supply.

Is the company's warehouse big enough? The paper will come on rolls, but to make the estimates easy, assume it is stacked. If it were stacked 10 feet high, the supply would require 100,000 square feet of floor space. The company's 14,000 square foot storage facility will probably not be big enough as its size differs by almost an order of magnitude from the estimate. The circulation estimate and the size of the newspaper estimate should each be within a factor of 2, implying that the 100,000 square foot estimate is off by at most a factor of 4—less than an order of magnitude.

How big a warehouse is needed? An acre is 43,560 square feet so about two acres of land is needed. Alternatively, a warehouse measuring 300 ft $\times$ 300 ft (the length of a football field in both directions) would contain 90,000 square feet of floor space, giving a rough idea of the size.

EXTENSIONS. After gaining some experience with these types of problems, students can be encouraged to pay close atten-

tion to the units and to be ready to make and support claims about the accuracy of their estimates. Paying attention to units and including units as algebraic quantities in calculations is a common technique in engineering and the sciences. Reasoning about a formula by paying attention only to the units is called dimensional analysis.

Sometimes, rather than a single estimate, it is helpful to make estimates of upper and lower bounds. Such an approach reinforces the idea that an exact answer is not the goal. In many situations, students could first estimate upper and lower bounds, and then collect some real data to determine whether the answer lies between those bounds. In the traditional game of guessing the number of jelly beans in a jar, for example, all students should be able to estimate within an order of magnitude, or perhaps within a factor of two. Making the closest guess, however, involves some chance.

Fermi questions are useful outside the workplace. Some Fermi questions have political ramifications:

● How many miles of streets are in your city or town? The police chief is considering increasing police presence so that every street is patrolled by car at least once every 4 hours.

● When will your town fill up its landfill? Is this a very urgent matter for the town's waste management personnel to assess in depth?

● In his 1997 State of the Union address, President Clinton renewed his call for a tax deduction of up to $10,000 for the cost of college tuition. He estimates that 16.5 million students stand to benefit. Is this a reasonable estimate of the number who might take advantage of the tax deduction? How much will the deduction cost in lost federal revenue?

Creating Fermi problems is easy. Simply ask quantitative questions for which there is no practical way to determine exact values. Students could be encouraged to make up their own. Examples are: "How many oak trees are there in Illinois?" or "How many people in the U.S. ate chicken for dinner last night?" "If all the people in the world were to jump in the ocean, how much would it raise the water level?" Give students the opportunity to develop their own Fermi problems and to share them with each other. It can stimulate some real mathematical thinking.

SCHEDULING ELEVATORS

TASK. In some buildings, all of the elevators can travel to all of the floors, while in others the elevators are restricted to stopping only on certain floors. What is the advantage of having elevators that travel only to certain floors? When is this worth instituting?

COMMENTARY. Scheduling elevators is a common example of an optimization problem that has applications in all aspects of business and industry. Optimal scheduling in general not only can save time and money, but it can contribute to safety (e.g., in the airline industry). The elevator problem further illustrates an important feature of many economic and political arguments— the dilemma of trying simultaneously to optimize several different needs.

Politicians often promise policies that will be the least expensive, save the most lives, and be best for the environment. Think of flood control or occupational safety rules, for example. When we are lucky, we can perhaps find a strategy of least cost, a strategy that saves the most lives, or a strategy that damages the environment least. But these might not be the same strategies: generally one cannot simultaneously satisfy two or more independent optimization conditions. This is an important message for students to learn, in order to become better educated and more critical consumers and citizens.

In the elevator problem, customer satisfaction can be emphasized by minimizing the average elevator time (waiting plus riding) for employees in an office building. Minimizing wait-time during rush hours means delivering many people quickly, which might be accomplished by filling the elevators and making few stops. During off-peak hours,

however, minimizing wait-time means maximizing the availability of the elevators. There is no reason to believe that these two goals will yield the same strategy. Finding the best strategy for each is a mathematical problem; choosing one of the two strategies or a compromise strategy is a management decision, not a mathematical deduction.

This example serves to introduce a complex topic whose analysis is well within the range of high school students. Though the calculations require little more than arithmetic, the task puts a premium on the creation of reasonable alternative strategies. Students should recognize that some configurations (e.g., all but one elevator going to the top floor and the one going to all the others) do not merit consideration, while others are plausible. A systematic evaluation of all possible configurations is usually required to find the optimal solution. Such a systematic search of the possible solution space is important in many modeling situations where a formal optimal strategy is not known. Creating and evaluating reasonable strategies for the elevators is quite appropriate for high school student mathematics and lends itself well to thoughtful group effort. How do you invent new strategies? How do you know that you have considered all plausible strategies? These are mathematical questions, and they are especially amenable to group discussion.

Students should be able to use the techniques first developed in solving a simple case with only a few stories and a few elevators to address more realistic situations (e.g., 50 stories, five elevators). Using the results of a similar but simpler problem to model a more complicated problem is an important way to reason in mathematics. Students need to determine what data and variables are relevant. Start by establishing the kind of building—a hotel, an office building, an apartment building? How many people are on the different floors? What are their normal destinations (e.g., primarily the ground floor or, perhaps, a roof-top restaurant). What happens during rush hours?

To be successful at the elevator task, students must first develop a mathematical model of the problem. The model might be a graphical representation for each elevator, with time on the horizontal axis and the floors represented on the vertical axis, or a tabular representation indicating the time spent on each floor. Students must identify the pertinent variables and make simplifying assumptions about which of the possible floors an elevator will visit.

MATHEMATICAL ANALYSIS. This section works through some of the details in a particularly simple case. Consider an office building with six occupied floors, employing 240 people, and a ground floor that is not used for business. Suppose there are three elevators, each of which can hold 10 people. Further suppose that each elevator takes approximately 25 seconds to fill on the ground floor, then takes 5 seconds to move between floors and 15 seconds to open and close at each floor on which it stops.

Scenario one. What happens in the morning when everyone arrives for work? Assume that everyone arrives at approximately the same time and enters the elevators on the ground floor. If all elevators go to all floors and if the 240 people are evenly divided among all three elevators, each elevator will have to make 8 trips of 10 people each.

When considering a single trip of one elevator, assume for simplicity that 10 people get on the elevator at the ground floor and that it stops at each floor on the way up, because there may be an occupant heading to each floor. Adding 5 seconds to move to each floor and 15 seconds to stop yields 20 seconds for each of the six floors. On the way down, since no one is being picked up or let off, the elevator does not stop, taking 5 seconds for each of six floors for a total of 30 seconds. This round-trip is represented in Table 1.

TABLE 1: Elevator round-trip time, Scenario one	TIME (SEC)
Ground Floor	25
Floor 1	20
Floor 2	20
Floor 3	20
Floor 4	20
Floor 5	20
Floor 6	20
Return	30
ROUND-TRIP	175

Since each elevator makes 8 trips, the total time will be 1,400 seconds or 23 minutes, 20 seconds.

Scenario two. Now suppose that one elevator serves floors 1–3 and, because of the longer trip, two elevators are assigned to floors 4–6. The elevators serving the top

TABLE 2: Elevator round-trip times, Scenario two			
	ELEVATOR A		**ELEVATORS B & C**
	STOP	TIME	STOP	TIME
Ground Floor		25		25
Floor 1	1	20		5
Floor 2	2	20		5
Floor 3	3	20		5
Floor 4		0	4	20
Floor 5		0	5	20
Floor 6		0	6	20
Return		15		30
ROUND-TRIP		100		130

in a small time savings (about 3 minutes) over the first scenario. Because elevators B and C are finished so much sooner than elevator A, there is likely a more efficient solution.

Scenario three. The two round-trip times in Table 2 do not differ by much because the elevators move quickly between floors but stop at floors relatively slowly. This observation suggests that a more efficient arrangement might be to assign each elevator to a pair of floors. The times for such a scenario are listed in Table 3.

Again assuming 40 employees per floor, each elevator will deliver 80 people, requiring 8 trips, taking at most a total of 920 seconds. Thus this assignment of elevators results in a time savings of almost 35% when compared with the 1400 seconds it would take to deliver all employees via unassigned elevators.

floors will save 15 seconds for each of floors 1–3 by not stopping. The elevator serving the bottom floors will save 20 seconds for each of the top floors and will save time on the return trip as well. The times for these trips are shown in Table 2.

Assuming the employees are evenly distributed among the floors (40 people per floor), elevator A will transport 120 people, requiring 12 trips, and elevators B and C will transport 120 people, requiring 6 trips each. These trips will take 1200 seconds (20 minutes) for elevator A and 780 seconds (13 minutes) for elevators B and C, resulting

TABLE 3: Elevator round-trip times, Scenario three						
	ELEVATOR A		**ELEVATOR B**		**ELEVATOR C**	
	STOP	TIME	STOP	TIME	STOP	TIME
Ground Floor		25		25		25
Floor 1	1	20		5		5
Floor 2	2	20		5		5
Floor 3		0	3	20		5
Floor 4		0	4	20		5
Floor 5		0		0	5	20
Floor 6		0		0	6	20
Return		10		20		30
ROUND-TRIP		75		95		115

Perhaps this is the optimal solution. If so, then the above analysis of this simple case suggests two hypotheses:

1. The optimal solution assigns each floor to a single elevator.

2. If the time for stopping is sufficiently larger than the time for moving between floors, each elevator should serve the same number of floors.

Mathematically, one could try to show that this solution is optimal by trying all possible elevator assignments or by carefully reasoning, perhaps by showing that the above hypotheses are correct. Practically, however, it doesn't matter because this solution considers only the morning rush hour and ignores periods of low use.

The assignment is clearly not optimal during periods of low use, and much of the inefficiency is related to the first hypothesis for rush hour optimization: that each floor is served by a single elevator. With this condition, if an employee on floor 6 arrives at the ground floor just after elevator C has departed, for example, she or he will have to wait nearly two minutes for elevator C to return, even if elevators A and B are idle. There are other inefficiencies that are not considered by focusing on the rush hour. Because each floor is served by a single elevator, an employee who wishes to travel from floor 3 to floor 6, for example, must go via the ground floor and switch elevators. Most employees would prefer more flexibility than a single elevator serving each floor.

At times when the elevators are not all busy, unassigned elevators will provide the quickest response and the greatest flexibility.

Because this optimal solution conflicts with the optimal rush hour solution, some compromise is necessary. In this simple case, perhaps elevator A could serve all floors, elevator B could serve floors 1-3, and elevator C could serve floors 4-6.

The second hypothesis, above, deserves some further thought. The efficiency of the rush hour solution Table 3 is due in part to the even division of employees among the floors. If employees were unevenly distributed with, say, 120 of the 240 people working on the top two floors, then elevator C would need to make 12 trips, taking a total of 1380 seconds, resulting in almost no benefit over unassigned elevators. Thus, an efficient solution in an actual building must take into account the distribution of the employees among the floors.

Because the stopping time on each floor is three times as large as the traveling time between floors (15 seconds versus 5 seconds), this solution effectively ignores the traveling time by assigning the same number of employees to each elevator. For taller buildings, the traveling time will become more significant. In those cases fewer employees should be assigned to the elevators that serve the upper floors than are assigned to the elevators that serve the lower floors.

EXTENSIONS. The problem can be made more challenging by altering the number of elevators, the number of floors, and the number of individuals working on each floor. The rate of movement of elevators can be determined by observing buildings in the local area. Some elevators move more quickly than others. Entrance and exit times could also be measured by students collecting data on local elevators. In a similar manner, the number of workers, elevators, and floors could be taken from local contexts.

A related question is, where should the elevators go when not in use? Is it best for them to return to the ground floor? Should they remain where they were last sent? Should they distribute themselves evenly among the floors? Or should they go to floors of anticipated heavy traffic? The answers will depend on the nature of the building and the time of day. Without analysis, it will not be at all clear which strategy is best under specific conditions. In some buildings, the elevators are controlled by computer programs that "learn" and then anticipate the traffic patterns in the building.

A different example that students can easily explore in detail is the problem of situating a fire station or an emergency room in a city. Here the key issue concerns travel times to the region being served, with conflicting optimization goals: average time vs. maximum time. A location that minimizes the maximum time of response may not produce the least average time of response. Commuters often face similar choices in selecting routes to work. They may want to minimize the average time, the maximum time, or perhaps the variance, so that their departure and arrival times are more predictable.

Most of the optimization conditions discussed so far have been expressed in units of time. Sometimes, however, two optimization conditions yield strategies whose outcomes are expressed in different (and sometimes incompatible) units of measurement. In many public policy issues (e.g., health insurance) the units are lives and money. For environmental issues, sometimes the units themselves are difficult to identify (e.g., quality of life).

When one of the units is money, it is easy to find expensive strategies but impossible to find ones that have virtually no cost. In some situations, such as airline safety, which balances lives versus dollars, there is no strategy that minimize lives lost (since additional dollars always produce slight increases in safety), and the strategy that minimizes dollars will be at $0. Clearly some compromise is necessary. Working with models of different solutions can help students understand the consequences of some of the compromises.

HEATING-DEGREE-DAYS

TASK. An energy consulting firm that recommends and installs insulation and similar energy saving devices has received a complaint from a customer. Last summer she paid $540 to insulate her attic on the prediction that it would save 10% on her natural gas bills. Her gas bills have been higher than the previous winter, however, and now she wants a refund on the cost of the insulation. She admits that this winter has been colder than the last, but she had expected still to see some savings.

The facts: This winter the customer has used 1,102 therms, whereas last winter she used only 1,054 therms. This winter has been colder: 5,101 heating-degree-days this winter compared to 4,201 heating-degree-days last winter. (See explanation below.) How does a representative of the energy consulting firm explain to this customer that the accumulated heating-degree-days measure how much colder this winter has been, and then explain how to calculate her anticipated versus her actual savings.

COMMENTARY. Explaining the mathematics behind a situation can be challenging and requires a real knowledge of the context, the procedures, and the underlying mathematical concepts. Such communication of mathematical ideas is a powerful learning device for students of mathematics as well as an important skill for the workplace. Though the procedure for this problem involves only proportions, a thorough explanation of the mathematics behind the procedure requires understanding of linear modeling and related algebraic reasoning, accumulation and other precursors of calculus, as well as an understanding of energy usage in home heating.

MATHEMATICAL ANALYSIS. The customer seems to understand that a straight comparison of gas usage does not take into account the added costs of colder weather, which can be significant. But before calculating any anticipated or actual savings, the customer needs some understanding of heating-degree-days. For many years, weather services and oil and gas companies have been using heating-degree-days to explain and predict energy usage and to measure energy savings of insulation and other devices. Similar degree-day units are also used in studying insect populations and crop growth. The concept provides a simple measure of the accumulated amount of cold or warm weather over time. In the discussion that follows, all temperatures are given in degrees Fahrenheit, although the process is equally workable using degrees Celsius.

Suppose, for example, that the minimum temperature in a city on a given day is 52 degrees and the maximum temperature is 64 degrees. The average temperature for the day is then taken to be 58 degrees. Subtracting that result from 65 degrees (the cutoff point for heating), yields 7 heating-degree-days for the day. By recording high and low temperatures and computing their average each day, heating-degree-days can be accumulated over the course of a month, a winter, or any period of time as a measure of the coldness of that period.

Over five consecutive days, for example, if the average temperatures were 58, 50, 60, 67, and 56 degrees Fahrenheit, the calculation yields 7, 15, 5, 0, and 9 heating-degree-days respectively, for a total accumulation of 36 heating-degree-days for the five days. Note that the fourth day contributes 0 heating-degree-days to the total because the temperature was above 65 degrees.

The relationship between average temperatures and heating-degree-days is represented graphically in Figure 1. The average temperatures are shown along the solid line graph. The area of each shaded rectangle represents the number of heating-degree-days for that day, because the width of each rectangle is one day and the height of each rectangle is the number of degrees below 65 degrees. Over time, the sum of the areas of the rectangles represents the number of heating-degree-days accumulated during the period. (Teachers of calculus will recognize connections between these ideas and integral calculus.)

The statement that accumulated heating-degree-days should be proportional to gas or heating oil usage is based primarily on two assumptions: first, on a day for which the average temperature is above 65 degrees, no heating should be required, and therefore there should be no gas or heating oil usage; second, a day for which the average temperature is 25 degrees (40 heating-degree-days) should require twice as much heating as a day for which the average temperature is 45

degrees (20 heating-degree-days) because there is twice the temperature difference from the 65 degree cutoff.

The first assumption is reasonable because most people would not turn on their heat if the temperature outside is above 65 degrees. The second assumption is consistent with Newton's law of cooling, which states that the rate at which an object cools is proportional to the difference in temperature between the object and its environment. That is, a house which is 40 degrees warmer than its environment will cool at twice the rate (and therefore consume energy at twice the rate to keep warm) of a house which is 20 degrees warmer than its environment.

The customer who accepts the heating-degree-day model as a measure of energy usage can compare this winter's usage with that of last winter. Because 5,101/4,201 = 1.21, this winter has been 21% colder than last winter, and therefore each house should require 21% more heat than last winter. If this customer hadn't installed the insulation, she would have required 21% more heat than last year, or about 1,275 therms. Instead, she has required only 5% more heat (1,102/1,054 = 1.05), yielding a savings of 14% off what would have been required (1,102/1,275 = .86).

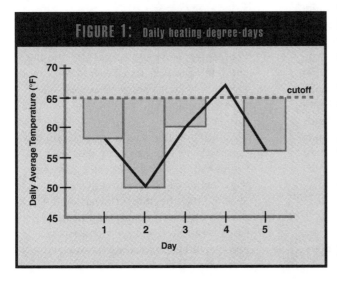

FIGURE 1: Daily heating-degree-days

Another approach to this would be to note that last year the customer used 1,054 therms/4,201 heating-degree-days = .251 therms/heating-degree-day, whereas this year she has used 1,102 therms/5,101 heating-degree-days = .216 therms/heating-degree-day, a savings of 14%, as before.

EXTENSIONS. How good is the heating-degree-day model in predicting energy usage? In a home that has a thermometer and a gas meter or a gauge on a tank, students could record daily data for gas usage and high and low temperature to test the accuracy of the model. Data collection would require only a few minutes per day for students using an electronic indoor/outdoor thermometer that tracks high and low temperatures. Of course, gas used for cooking and heating water needs to be taken into account. For homes in which the gas tank has no gauge or doesn't provide accurate enough data, a similar experiment could be performed relating accumulated heating-degree-days to gas or oil usage between fill-ups.

It turns out that in well-sealed modern houses, the cutoff temperature for heating can be lower than 65 degrees (sometimes as low as 55 degrees) because of heat generated by light bulbs, appliances, cooking, people, and pets. At temperatures sufficiently below the cutoff, linearity turns out to be a good assumption. Linear regression on the daily usage data (collected as suggested above) ought to find an equation something like $U = -.251(T - 65)$, where T is the average temperature and U is the gas usage. Note that the slope, $-.251$, is the gas usage per heating-degree-day, and 65 is the cutoff. Note also that the accumulation of heating-degree-days takes a linear equation and turns it into a proportion. There are some important data analysis issues that could be addressed by such an investigation. It is sometimes dangerous, for example, to assume linearity with only a few data points, yet this widely used model essentially assumes linearity from only one data point, the other point having coordinates of 65 degrees, 0 gas usage.

Over what range of temperatures, if any, is this a reasonable assumption? Is the standard method of computing average temperature a good method? If, for example, a day is mostly near 20 degrees but warms up to 50 degrees for a short time in the afternoon, is 35 heating-degree-days a good measure of the heating required that day? Computing averages of functions over time is a standard problem that can be solved with integral calculus. With knowledge of typical and extreme rates of temperature change, this could become a calculus problem or a problem for approximate solution by graphical methods without calculus, providing background experience for some of the important ideas in calculus.

Students could also investigate actual savings after insulating a home in their school district. A customer might typically see 8-10% savings for insulating roofs, although if the house is framed so that the walls act like chimneys, ducting air from the house and the basement into the attic, there might be very little savings. Eliminating significant leaks, on the other hand, can yield savings of as much as 25%.

Some U.S. Department of Energy studies discuss the relationship between heating-degree-days and performance and find the cutoff temperature to be lower in some modern houses. State energy offices also have useful documents.

What is the relationship between heating-degree-days computed using degrees Fahrenheit, as above, and heating-degree-days computed using degrees Celsius? Showing that the proper conversion is a direct proportion and not the standard Fahrenheit-Celsius conversion formula requires some careful and sophisticated mathematical thinking.

PART TWO

THE ROLES OF STANDARDS AND ASSESSMENTS

Overview

With President Clinton's call for voluntary national tests of reading in fourth grade and of mathematics in eighth grade, the debate about the role of the government in establishing standards and assessments has reached new heights on the political and educational landscapes. At the state level, debates about standards have been particularly heated in California, especially during the process of adopting state content and performance standards for all students. Throughout the country, much of the debate about standards has taken the form of dichotomies growing from language that positions opponents at extreme ends of the spectrum, arising particularly from opposing views about how people learn mathematics. For example, must automaticity with procedural skills precede any problem solving, or should thinking and reasoning permeate all aspects of the discipline, even before focusing on skill development? Although resolving these issues is beyond the scope of this document, finding common ground that transcends these dichotomies is a challenging but necessary part of the process of developing standards.

From any perspective in the standards debate, and from any political position, the call for standards is born, in part, out of parents' concerns for their children's futures: What should my child be learning? What should my child know in order to be admitted to a good college or university? What should my child know in order to get a good job? One of the main themes of this document—that problems from the workplace and everyday life can enhance the mathematical education of all students—implies the fortunate conclusion that the answers to these questions need not conflict.

Discussion of national standards has a long history. The release of *A Nation at Risk* (National Commission on Excellence in Education, 1983) had an effect like that of national standards, for many high schools responded by increasing their course requirements for graduation. Since then, many organizations concerned with different aspects of education have released documents delineating standards. In 1989, the National Council of Teachers of Mathematics (NCTM) published *Curriculum and Evaluation Standards for School Mathematics*. More recently, many states have produced or are producing frameworks describing new goals for K-12 performance and instruction in mathematics as well as other disciplines. Some of those states have also produced state-wide assessments that are explicitly aligned with those frameworks. At the national level, the Secretary's Commission on Achieving Necessary Skills (SCANS) described competencies needed for careers in its 1991 report, *What Work Requires of Schools*. The Goals 2000: Educate America Act established the National Skill Standards Board in 1994 to serve as a catalyst in the development of a voluntary national system of skills standards, assessments, and certifications for business and industry. In science, the American Association for the Advancement of Science (AAAS) developed *Benchmarks for Science Literacy* (AAAS, 1993). After four years of development, consensus-building, and extensive formal review, the National Research Council (NRC) contributed the *National Science Education Standards* (NRC, 1996). Also in 1995, the American Mathematical Association of Two-Year Colleges published *Crossroads in Mathematics: Standards for Introductory Mathematics Before Calculus*.

With so many voices contributing standards and recommendations, teachers are faced with difficult challenges. Despite the fact that the meaning of the word "standard" varies greatly among and even within the above documents— from statements about values to visions of the future; from statements about goals or expectations to criteria for evaluation—nevertheless, some common themes emerge. The standards for mathematics and those for science, for example, have many commonalities, as Jane Butler Kahle discusses in her essay, including ideas such as problem solving and communication.

The SCANS requirements for the workplace, described in Arnold Packer's essay, also emphasize problem solving and communication, but these skills are embedded in a framework that is hard to reconcile with the traditional division of schooling into subject areas. In particular, the SCANS requirements for Planning Skills, Interpersonal Skills, and Personal Qualities, do not fall under any of the traditional grades 9-12 subject headings and are rarely explicitly discussed as part of the curriculum, especially in mathematics. How might such skills might be developed in a mathematics class? Part of an answer lies in the

SCANS Commission's belief that the requirements should be taught in context. Throughout the nation, calls for new standards, new pedagogy, or new curricula often meet with a challenge: But how will students do on standardized tests? Discussions of student achievement as measured by standardized tests often misses two important questions: For what purpose was the test designed? And what is the relationship between this test and the educational goals that I value? The NCTM *Assessment Standards* (NCTM, 1995) describe four purposes of assessment: monitoring students' progress, making instructional decisions, evaluating students' achievement, and evaluating programs. Though the relationship between standards and assessments often goes unarticulated in public discussions, a constructive discussion of changes in mathematics education must carefully consider the roles of the assessment tools in place, some of which function as implicit standards because they influence expectations about what counts mathematically. Because the SAT and the ACT have come to serve gatekeeping functions in college admissions and in scholarship decisions, they influence the ideas of parents and policy makers alike about what constitutes desirable mathematical performance. The ACT purports to measure the academic skills that students will need to perform college-level work. Based upon what is taught in the high school curriculum, and requiring integration of knowledge from a variety of courses, the ACT Assessment tests are designed to determine how well students solve problems, grasp implied meanings, draw inferences, evaluate ideas, and make judgments. The SAT aims to measure verbal and mathematical reasoning abilities. Both tests are intended as predictors of success in college (in particular, in the first year of college); they attempt to fulfill a necessary function: providing colleges with a metric that allows for comparison of students from different schools when grades might not be comparable.

But how do SAT and ACT scores compare with other measurements of mathematical performance? Can a test like the SAT adequately assess learning when the curriculum emphasizes extended, open-ended, or collaborative tasks? William Linder-Scholer poses these questions in his essay and suggests a data-analysis task for parents: assessing the SAT as a measurement of student achievement and school quality, and as a basis for comparing education in different states.

Though Linder-Scholer's essay provides some understanding of the difficulties in comparing average test scores for schools or states, many important questions are left unaddressed. Serious consideration of the role of college entrance exams depends upon answers to two perennial questions: What do colleges, parents, and scholarship organizations do with the individual scores from these tests? And does the SAT measure what colleges value? Both the ACT and the SAT have evolved over the years to better serve the needs of parents, colleges, and schools. Nonetheless, these questions require ongoing research in response to changing curricula in high schools and colleges, and in response to the changing needs of colleges and the workplace. Constructive evolution of the role of college entrance exams requires collective deliberations among parents, teachers, college representatives, and testing experts around what these tests should be and how they may be used most effectively.

In his essay, John Dossey provides an international perspective on the character of the examinations given to students between high school and college. Looking at such examinations in the United States, England, Wales, and four European countries, he finds that contextualized, extended-response tasks are not routinely included. Such tasks are included, however, on the National Assessment of Educational Progress (NAEP), which provides national and state indicators about mathematics education but no individual scores (see, e.g., Reese et al., 1997). The NAEP results indicate that if such tasks are to assess individual student learning, "students will need a great deal of support in formulating, solving, and communicating their results."

The tasks that accompany these essays serve as examples and illustrations of tasks that might help provide that support. Well-chosen tasks are in no way to be construed as standards, but instead provide opportunities for building understanding of the mathematical ideas that are embodied in standards.

Mental Mathematics (p. 83) suggests ways that mental arithmetic and algebra might each contribute to the other. Though **Buying on Credit** (p. 87) is about finance and **Drug Dosage** (p. 80) is about pharmacology, the mathematics behind the tasks is quite similar, involving rates, series, and recursion. Despite the similar mathematical content of the two tasks, both are included to suggest an opportunity for students to engage in mathematical thinking: to describe and understand whole classes of tasks by noticing commonalities among their procedures or representations. The similarity, after all, can be clear only with sufficient mathematical understanding of multiple contexts.

REFERENCES

American Association for the Advancement of Science. (1993). *Benchmarks for science literacy.* Washington, DC: Author.

American Mathematical Association of Two-Year Colleges (1995). *Crossroads in mathematics: Standards for introductory college mathematics before calculus.* Memphis, TN: Author.

National Commission on Excellence in Education. (1983). *A nation at risk: The imperative for educational reform.* Washington, DC: Author.

National Council of Teachers of Mathematics. (1989). *Curriculum and evaluation standards for school mathematics.* Reston, VA: Author.

National Council of Teachers of Mathematics. (1995). *Assessment standards for school mathematics.* Reston, VA: Author.

National Research Council. (1996). *National science education standards.* Washington, DC: National Academy Press.

Reese, C. M., Miller, K. E., Mazzeo, J., & Dossey, J. A. (1997). *NAEP 1996 mathematics report card for the nation and the states.* Washington, DC: National Center for Education Statistics.

United States Department of Labor. Secretary's Commission on Achieving Necessary Skills. (1991). *What work requires of schools: A SCANS report for America 2000.* Washington, DC: Author.

6 Science and Mathematics Education: Finding Common Ground

Jane Butler Kahle
Miami University

The current reforms in both science and mathematics education have many commonalities; in fact, for the first time, the two disciplines are advancing with common goals and objectives, as evidenced in the mathematics standards published by the National Council of Teachers of Mathematics (NCTM, 1989, 1991, 1995), and the science standards published by the National Research Council (NRC, 1996). Both sets of standards are based on the premises that all children can learn challenging mathematics and science, that literacy in both disciplines is necessary for productive work in the future, that learners construct their own knowledge, and that there are many effective ways to promote knowledge construction.

One way to elaborate such standards is to provide tasks that illustrate some of the ideas promoted by those standards. Tasks that fit with these standards have common characteristics: they require time, they allow multiple solution paths, they are open-ended, they may be revisited and extended, and they develop basic skills. Individually, each characteristic is applicable to both science and mathematics; and collectively, these characteristics delineate a practical route from the rhetoric of standards to the reality of student achievement. Many of the skills involved in doing these tasks are critical to success in the sciences, as well as in mathematics.

Useful and compelling mathematics tasks illustrate both the logical and algorithmic nature of mathematics as well as its whimsy and beauty. These dual goals again make a connection with science. A national study of mine (Kahle, 1983) indicated that both ninth- and tenth-grade girls and boys were motivated to continue to study advanced science when their science teachers stressed both the basic skills of science (many of which may be learned in mathematics) and its more creative elements. I believe that problems that illustrate the whimsy and beauty of mathematics will encourage and excite many students who heretofore have been turned off to mathematics.

Mathematics instruction that fits with the NCTM *Standards* includes tasks that actively engage students in making meaning of mathematics and in proposing several possible solution processes. Such activities provide sites in which the NCTM process standards—mathematics as problem solving, mathematics as communication, mathematics as reasoning, and mathematical connections—can be emphasized and developed.

Science instruction consistent with the *National Science Education Standards* (*NSES*) (NRC, 1996) is characterized by similar parameters: students identify a problem from their observations of nature; they propose several solutions (hypotheses); in any one class, their investigations take multiple approaches; and they discuss and consider all reasonable solutions. The science as inquiry standards in particular promote the following processes:

> . . . asking questions, planning and conducting investigations, using appropriate tools and techniques to gather data, thinking critically and logically about relationships between evidence and explanations, constructing and analyzing alternative explanations, and communicating scientific arguments. (NRC, 1996, p. 105)

Practically speaking, it is possible to write tasks that are directly applicable to both mathematics and science lessons. In this volume, **Drug Dosage** (p. 80) is a task in which students may either use a mathematical model to understand a scientific context or use a scientific context to understand mathematical ideas in the model. Because of their availability and low cost, paper towels are a common context for tasks that integrate mathematics and science[1]. In order to compare brands for absorbency, strength when wet, or cost per sheet, or to investigate concepts such as the relationship between the number of water drops absorbed by the towel and the area of the wet spot, students design experiments and collect and interpret data.

The *NSES* includes an excellent example of an activity, "The Solar System," for an integrated mathematics and science program (NRC, 1996, pp. 215-217). The goal of the activity is to have students construct a scale model of the sun, moon, and earth using techniques developed by early astronomers. Students observe the stars, discuss the patterns they observe, and use a particular pattern (the North Star, Polaris, doesn't appear to move) to suggest methods for estimating the circumference of the earth. In particular, if they know angle of the North Star at two locations on the same longitude and a known distance apart, they may estimate the circumference of the earth by using a two-dimensional diagram of the three-dimensional situation (see Figure 6-1), and by using geometric knowledge about circles, tangents, and angles. Through activities such as this, students can see not only that geometric understanding is necessary to understand the science problem, but also that science provides contexts for geometric and mathematical ideas.

These possibilities arise because of common skills that are needed to study both mathematics and science. For example, in both disciplines, students need to be able to estimate, to use mathematical models, to interpolate and extrapolate, to identify false negatives, to detect bias, to convert two-dimensional drawings to three-dimensional models and vice versa, to make and interpret graphs and other diagrams, and so on. Furthermore, when students use data gathered in science investigations in their mathematics courses, they encounter many of the anomalies of authentic data: inconsistencies, outliers, and errors. Indeed, tasks that build these kinds of skills are good examples of activities through which it should be possible to develop aspects of the scientific literacy stressed in the *NSES* (NRC, 1996), as well as the mathematical understandings promoted in the NCTM's *Curriculum and Evaluation Standards for School Mathematics* (NCTM, 1989).

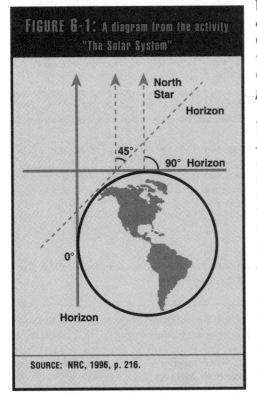

FIGURE 6-1: A diagram from the activity "The Solar System"

SOURCE: NRC, 1996, p. 216.

Because of these connections between mathematics and science, the *NSES* calls for coordinating the science and mathematics programs in schools. Such coordination results in opportunities to advance instruction in science beyond purely descriptive studies and to provide mathematics classes with authentic problems. The NCTM *Standards* documents (NCTM, 1989, 1991, 1995) also clearly encourage making connections between mathematics and the sciences, particularly in the sections on mathematical connections. The documents note the pervasiveness of the connections between mathematics and other disciplines and encourage such connections in the classroom as a means of enabling students to see the utility of mathematics and to find motivation for mathematics.

We have been singularly unsuccessful in developing a long-term relationship, let alone a successful marriage, between science and mathematics as they are usually taught in schools. An often-promoted solution is simply using science examples in mathematical problems. This solution is too simple, obviously, and has not been successful in the past. However, both the *NSES* and this volume provide glimpses of what will work. First, students need to be able to integrate the scientific skills of observing, classifying, inferring, collecting, and interpreting data, using mathematical skills such as reasoning, computing, communicating, and making connections. For all students, the process of doing both good science and good mathematics holds the most promise of successful integration, an integration constructed by each learner as her or his skills and understandings develop. *Mathematics at Work* may help inspire a future in which value is placed upon the processes, not products, of learning, where science and mathematics are integrated through common skills, where relevant activities that integrate mathematics and science are readily available for each student, and where the common ground that is shared by those interested in high-quality mathematics and science education is explicit.

REFERENCES

Kahle, J. B. (Ed.). (1983). *Girls in school: Women in science*. Washington, DC: National Science Board, Commission on Precollege Education in Mathematics. (ERIC Document Reproduction Service No. ED 258 812).

National Council of Teachers of Mathematics. (1989). *Curriculum and evaluation standards for school mathematics*. Reston, VA: Author.

National Council of Teachers of Mathematics. (1991). *Professional standards for teaching mathematics*. Reston, VA: Author.

National Council of Teachers of Mathematics. (1995). *Assessment standards for school mathematics*. Reston, VA: Author.

National Research Council. (1996). *National science education standards*. Washington, DC: National Academy Press.

Sneider, C. I. & Barber, J. (1987). *Paper towel testing*. Great Explorations in Math and Science (GEMS) Project. Berkeley, CA: Lawrence Hall of Science, University of California, Berkeley.

Teaching Integrated Mathematics and Science (TIMS) Project, Inc. (1992). *Spreading Out II*. Chicago: University of Illinois at Chicago.

NOTE

1. See, for example, *Spreading Out II* (Teaching Integrated Mathematics and Science (TIMS) Project, Inc. 1992) and *Paper Towel Testing* (Sneider & Barber, 1987).

JANE BUTLER KAHLE is Conduit Professor of Science Education at Miami University. She is Chair of the Committee on Science Education, K-12. She has been President of the National Association of Biology Teachers and the National Association for Research in Science Teaching as well as Chair of National Science Foundation's Committee on Equal Opportunities in Science and Engineering and Biological Sciences Curriculum Studies' (BSCS) Board of Directors.

7 SCANS AND MATHEMATICS— SUPPORTING THE TRANSITION FROM SCHOOLS TO CAREERS

ARNOLD PACKER
JOHNS HOPKINS UNIVERSITY

This essay addresses two related questions: What kinds of tasks will support the learning of "SCANS" skills described by the report entitled *What Work Requires of Schools* (United States Department of Labor, 1991)? And will use of such tasks facilitate student success in making the transition from school to career?

The charge of the Secretary's Commission on Achieving Necessary Skills (SCANS) was to examine the demands of the workplace and whether students were being prepared to meet those demands. SCANS commissioned a variety of studies. Six special panels examined jobs ranging from manufacturing to government employment. Researchers interviewed a wide range of workers. The commission itself met with business owners, employers, union representatives, and workers. In summarizing the findings of these studies, the SCANS report describes five sets of competencies and a three-part foundation of skills and attributes essential for all students, both those going directly to work and those planning further education. The commission believes that, in line with current research in cognitive science, the eight requirements should be taught in context rather than as abstract concepts and skills to be applied later.

The five competencies are

- *Planning Skills,* such as allocating time, money, space, and staff;

- *Interpersonal Skills*, such as negotiating and teaching;

- *Information Skills*, such as acquiring, evaluating, interpreting, and communicating information;

- *Technology Skills*, such as selecting, using, and fixing technology; and

- *Systems Skills*, such as understanding, improving, and designing systems.

For example, an entry-level restaurant worker should be able to estimate costs of replacing equipment and justify necessary expenses in writing. In order to plan where the equipment should be placed, the worker should be capable of reading blueprints and manufacturers' installation requirements. Such a worker might need interpersonal skills to explain technology or scheduling to a new employee, for example. A necessary information skill might include being able to use a spread-sheet program to estimate the costs of food required for different menus. And the worker should be able to analyze and modify the system, determining the average and maximum amount of time a customer waits between ordering and receiving an appetizer, and between receiving an appetizer and the entree.

In this example, aspects of the three-part foundation of attributes and skills are intertwined with the five competencies. The three-part foundation consists of

- *Basic Skills,* such as reading, writing, and computing;

- *Thinking Skills*, such as visualization, reasoning, and the ability to solve problems; and

- *Personal Qualities*, such as perseverance, politeness, self-esteem, and empathy.

In the restaurant scenario above, the worker needs to read blueprints, write a justification, and compute costs. Planning where to place equipment requires processing the information from the blueprints as well as the information given about the dimensions of the equipment. Throughout this scenario, politeness is necessary, in directing workers where to place equipment, in explaining matters to a new worker, and, of course, in dealing with customers.

What Work Requires of Schools describes these attributes and skills as both extensive and enduring. They are extensive because they are needed at all stages of careers of all kinds, including careers that require post-graduate education, and they are enduring because these skills have been needed for centuries and will be needed for centuries to come. Furthermore, the report claims that any authentic workplace task requiring a high level of effort and perseverance will necessarily involve one or more of the five competencies.

When designing tasks to serve the SCANS goals, one needs to consider tasks likely to be encountered in the workplace. From the SCANS perspective, a good task is one that a million or more workers in the U.S. economy are being paid to solve. (This is not to disparage tasks that students will need to solve in roles outside the workplace, such as citizenship or parenting. But in SCANS, workplace issues predominate.)

The most important worker in the educational system is the student. Recent surveys of jobs by the SCANS Commission, by American College Testing, and by the American Institute for Research (for O*NET) indicate that students need a firm grasp of applied algebra—not a vague understanding of calculus (Packer, 1997). They can always look up algorithms and formulas in order to solve a quadratic equation or complete a square. Even if students can recall them to pass their final exams, they are likely to forget many algorithms and formulas two weeks later. What they need to demonstrate on exams is that they know how to bring mathematics to bear on SCANS-like problems such as budgeting and scheduling.

The issue has become more important because President Clinton has called for a national 8th grade mathematics assessment. Should the test pose mathematical "puzzles" that are interesting to the mathematically inclined? Or should test items have a clear relationship to problems that students are likely to encounter outside the schoolroom walls?

The SCANS goals require more variety in the circumstances under which tasks are done. The traditional problem archetypes, such as canoe problems and train problems, also have a traditional format—they are done individually in 10 minutes or less. In contrast, the SCANS competencies of teaching, negotiating, interpreting, and communicating require tasks that can only be solved collectively by groups. All of these changes will help schools reflect the needs of the workplace with greater accuracy and ease the transition from schools to careers.

REFERENCES

United States Department of Labor. Secretary's Commission on Achieving Necessary Skills. (1991). *What work requires of schools: A SCANS report for America 2000*. Washington, DC: Author.

Packer, A. (1997). Mathematical Competencies That Employers Expect. In L.A. Steen (Ed.), *Why numbers count: Quantitative literacy for tomorrow's America*, (pp. 137-154). New York: College Entrance Examination Board.

ARNOLD PACKER is a Senior Fellow at the Institute for Policy Studies of Johns Hopkins University. He was Executive Director of the Secretary's Commission on Achieving Necessary Skills (SCANS) and co-author of Workforce 2000. He has served as Assistant Secretary at the U.S. Department of Labor, and as first Chief Economist at the U.S. Senate Budget Committee. He is a licensed (and practicing) engineer in New York and California. His Ph.D. in Economics is from University of North Carolina at Chapel Hill.

8 Thinking About the SAT

William Linder-Scholer

SciMath Minnesota

For many parents, standardized test scores seem to answer the basic questions about education that everyone asks: How good is the school my child attends? How do the schools in our state or region compare with schools elsewhere? What chance does my son or daughter have of being admitted to a good college or university?

Schools commonly use achievement test results to determine whether students are making progress and to ensure that programs in basic subjects, such as mathematics and reading, are effective. The referendum-voting and home-buying public use test scores to judge the quality of their schools and the desirability of living in one community over another. Colleges often combine students' high school grade point averages and scores on standardized tests to make crucial in-or-out decisions about admissions.

But how reliable are standardized test results? Can we really use achievement test rankings or college-admissions test scores to make fair and meaningful comparisons of students, schools, and states?

Workplace and everyday tasks like those in this volume bring these questions into sharp relief in two very different ways. First, such tasks differ considerably from the tasks used in standardized tests, most notably in the time a student is expected to spend on the task and in what constitutes a solution.

This point raises questions about whether any standardized test can adequately assess a type of education in which extended tasks are used for instruction. Second, the kind of reasoning that parents need to gauge properly the significance of test score data is precisely the kind of reasoning that we might encourage. Interpreting test score data is itself a mathematical task!

INTERPRETING THE SAT

For better or worse, we know that Americans have been making the comparisons outlined above for generations. This fact is perhaps best illustrated by the power and popularity of the SAT[1]—the single most-used standardized test of its type in the country and an important ingredient in college admissions since the 1940s. The SAT I: Reasoning Test, a multiple-choice exam[2] with verbal and mathematics components, is used in combination with high school grades to predict a student's readiness for college. Fluctuations in average SAT scores are tracked as indicators, albeit indirect, of the quality of education in this country (Bracey, 1996; Powell & Steelman, 1996).

Beginning in 1964, average scores on the SAT dropped slowly but steadily for about 15 years. This led to much speculation and considerable hand-wringing about possible causes of the apparent decline in education quality in the U.S. By the early 1990s, average scores on the mathematics portion of the SAT had rebounded significantly, but scores on the verbal section had not.

Scores on other national standardized exams also declined during this same time period, but none attracted as much attention as the SAT. Further significance was attributed to this alarming drop in SAT scores by the many reports of poor mathematics and science performance by U.S. students relative to that of students in other countries. In the U.S., state-by-state comparisons of SAT results became a standard feature of the economic "warfare" among the states to lure businesses and their employees based on relative measures of "quality of life" as reflected in part by test-score rankings.

MISSING INFORMATION

The trouble with all of this is that test scores, particularly average scores on nationally-normed standardized tests such as the SAT, don't mean as much as we typically think they do. Understanding who takes the test—and who doesn't—is the first and perhaps single most important factor to consider when trying to understand what raw SAT scores or state-to-state comparisons really mean.

For starters, we need to know what percentage of students actually take the test. Students who take the SAT (or equivalent admissions exams such as the ACT, used more extensively in the Midwestern states) are obviously prospective college students and thus not representative of the total school population. Thirty years ago, average national scores on the SAT exam were highly unrepresentative of the achievement of the "average" student in the U.S. because the pool of candidates taking the test was much smaller than it is now. In fact, in 1975 SAT-takers included only one-third of the nation's graduating seniors, but by 1994, they included 42% of the nation's graduates (College Entrance Examination Board, 1994). Although experts disagree about specifics, the decline in SAT scores during the 1960s and 1970s seems due at least in part to the fact that the test-taking pool is formed of a larger percentage of high school graduates, and, thus, in the '60s and '70s, an average SAT-taker was more like an average high school graduate than was the case in the 1950s.

Today, with an even larger portion of total school population taking the SAT, we can more fairly make comparisons, yet in making state-to-state contrasts we must still account for differential rates of overall student participation. In 1993 for example, the average SAT score for students in Iowa was 1103. Students in Massachusetts averaged 903 (Powell & Steelman, 1996). But in Iowa only 5% of high school seniors took the SAT. In Massachusetts, participation was far greater—81% of high school seniors took the exam. Generally speaking, in states where SAT participation rates are relatively high, the likelihood is that average scores will be lower than in the low-participation states. (See Figure 8-1.)

However, who takes the test, as well as how many take it, also makes a difference in scores. To some extent, the diversification of the SAT-taking pool during the 1960s and 1970s was due to the overdue "democratization" of the test-taking group, with the addition to the SAT pool of significant numbers of female students and students of color, groups who previously had been underrepresented among the college-bound. Students in these groups often do not experience the "same" edu-

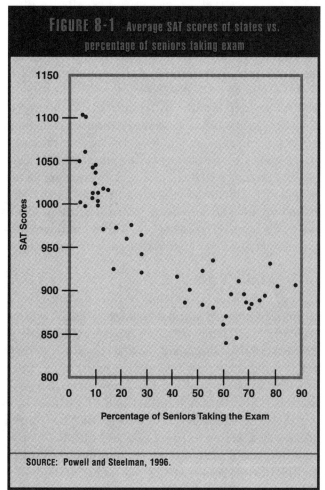

FIGURE 8-1 Average SAT scores of states vs. percentage of seniors taking exam

SAT Scores

Percentage of Seniors Taking the Exam

SOURCE: Powell and Steelman, 1996.

cation as those from groups who are traditionally expected to be college-bound (Oakes, 1990; Wellesley College Center for Research on Women, 1992).

But the effect of this democratization is not simple. Changes and rates of change in SAT scores are linked in complex ways to both how many students take the test and the composition of the test-taking pool. Consider the following facts that run counter to the common expectation that such democratization causes average scores to fall:

- During the 1970s, at the very time that SAT scores fell fastest, high school graduation rates were stable, the percentage of students taking the test changed very little, and the percentage of students going to college also changed only minimally. Clearly, other factors were at work in causing the test score declines.

- The most dramatic compositional changes in the SAT test-taking pool (particularly the increase in numbers of ethnic minority students) occurred after 1980, at a time when SAT scores were leveling off and beginning to head back up, especially in mathematics (College Entrance Examination Board, 1994).

Comparing states gets even more complicated when we consider the fact that SAT scores can also be influenced by differences in school environments. Low expectations for student performance, tracking of students into unchallenging academic programs, high student-teacher ratios, and differences in curricula and instructional practices account for significant differences in school performance and can also influence a state's SAT average. And, conversely, some changes in curriculum and instruction may not influence SAT averages. For example, the Interactive Mathematics Program (IMP) is a non-traditional high-school curriculum based on complex extended problems. The average SAT score for IMP students was only 1 point higher than that of a matched sample of students enrolled in a traditional mathematics curriculum. But 87 percent of IMP students took the SAT and only 58% of their counterparts did (Interactive Mathematics Program, 1995).

For reasons like these, the U.S. government long ago instituted the National Assessment of Educational Progress (NAEP), which tests a representative sampling of all high school students in the country, not just the college-bound. Although the NAEP does not adjust for state-to-state variation in expectations, curricula, and other environmental differences, it does test a representative sample of students on a range of tasks, which include SAT-like items as well as extended-response tasks. In this sense, it provides a more reliable way than the SAT of comparing one state's educational performance with another. In fact, a cross-check of the state-by-state NAEP results for grade 4 and grade 8 (White, 1993) is one way to put some "context" around SAT-score comparisons.

So here we have a mathematical task for parents and guardians. The calculations necessary for comparing one state's SAT scores with another's must include the percentage of total students taking the examination in each state as well as the composition of each pool and, secondarily, information regarding the relative strengths and weaknesses of the states based on existing measures of academic performance. Unlocking the mystery of test-score statistics means understanding raw numbers in the context of a host of student population and school environment factors. It means getting beyond the simplistic messages of test-score headlines in order to understand relative measures of student achievement and quality of the educational system.

REFERENCES

Bracey, G. W. (1996). Money improves test scores—even state-level SATs. *Phi Delta Kappan, 78*(1), 91-92.

Burton, N. (1996). Have changes in the SAT affected women's mathematics performance? *Educational Measurement: Issues and Practice, 15*(4), 5-9.

College Entrance Examination Board. (1994). *College-bound seniors: 1994 profile of SAT and achievement test takers*. Princeton, NJ: Educational Testing Service.

Interactive Mathematics Program. (1995). *Evaluation update*. Issue 1, 1995. (Available from 2420 Van Leyden Way, Modesto, CA 95356.)

Oakes, J. (1990). *Multiplying inequalities: The effects of race, social class, and tracking on opportunities to learn mathematics and science*. Santa Monica, CA: Rand Corporation.

Powell, B. & Steelman, L. C. (1996). Bewitched, bothered, and bewildering: The use and misuse of state SAT and ACT scores. *Harvard Educational Review, 66*(27-59).

Wellesley College Center for Research on Women. (1992). *How schools shortchange girls*. Washington, DC: American Association of University Women.

White, S. E. (1993). *NAEP 1992 mathematics report card for the nation and the states*. Washington, DC: National Center for Education Statistics.

NOTES

1. The SAT is not an acronym, but a registered trademark. Since 1994, the SAT program has consisted of the SAT I: Reasoning Test, formerly the Scholastic Aptitude Test, and SAT II: Subject Tests, formerly the Achievement Tests. Also in 1994, calculators became optional for the mathematics portions of the tests.
2. The mathematics section of the "old" SAT consisted of 60 multiple-choice questions, which were to be done within one hour thirty minutes (Interactive Mathematics Program, 1995). The mathematics section of the new SAT consists of 60 questions to be done within one hour and forty-five minutes. Fifty of the questions are multiple choice and 10 are "grid-ins" (Burton, 1996).

WILLIAM LINDER-SCHOLER is Executive Director of SciMathMN, a statewide public/private partnership that advocates standards-based reform for K-12 mathematics and science education in Minnesota. He is a member of the National Research Council's Committee on Science Education, K-12, and served on the committee which guided development of the National Research Council's *National Science Education Standards*. He is a member of the Executive Council of the National Association for State Science and Mathematics Coalitions. Linder-Scholer previously served as Director of Community Affairs at Cray Research, Inc., the Fortune-500 supercomputer company, and as Director of the Cray Research Philanthropic Foundation, where he directed a national grant-making program focused on mathematics and engineering education.

9 Extended Response Tasks in International Contexts

John Dossey
Illinois State University

Mathematical tasks with a strong connection to today's workplace call for students to use procedures drawing on knowledge of recursion, numerical approximations, exploratory data analysis, and statistical hypothesis testing. Such problems are realistic, authentic, and representative of the real world. They can involve a great deal of good mathematics. However, they can also be quite different from what one sees in the examinations given to high school students of other countries (Britton & Raizen, 1996; Dossey, 1996).

An International View

School-leaving examinations (given to all students at the end of high school) in England and Wales, France, Germany, Japan, Sweden, and even the United States, tend to focus much more on the narrow "taught curriculum" of traditionally conceived concepts and procedures related to the road to calculus—and to the university. This canon of work is generally limited to various forms of algebra, geometry, elementary functions (including trigonometry), and introductory calculus. An analysis of representative examinations from these countries for 1991 and 1992 (Dossey, 1996) indicates that the heaviest concentration of test items falls in the areas of calculus (applications of the definite integral, applications of the derivative, and the use of the derivative in finding maxima and minima), functions (interpreting the graphs of functions, trigonometric equations, and trigonometric identities), and probability distributions—notably, the normal distribution (also known as the bell curve) and its properties.

Little evidence was seen in the study of these school-leaving (or college-entrance) examinations of items that reflect rich ties to contemporary real-world problems. For example, when recursion appeared, it did so in a relationship between trigonometric functions or in the context of a radioactive substance which decayed exponentially, both rather theoretical settings. There were no tasks involving recursion as rich in contemporary connections as you will see in **Lottery Winnings** (p. 111), **Drug Dosage** (p. 80), or **Buying on Credit** (p. 87). In a like manner, no international evidence was seen of tasks concerning back-of-the-envelope calculations, estimation, rounding, or general number, operation, and symbol sense—all of which occur in various tasks in this volume.

The school-leaving and college-entrance examinations at the international level showed a strong predisposition to focus applications in one area: classical applications of mathematics to motion and mechanics problems from physics. Consider the following item taken from the 1991 University of Tokyo examination for students applying to enter the university in science. It presents a non-routine but classically oriented problem dealing with kinematics (Wu, 1993):

> Let a, b, and c be positive real numbers. In the xyz-space, consider the truncated plane R consisting of points (x, y, z) satisfying the conditions
>
> $$|x| \leq a, \ |y| \leq b, \text{ and } z = c.$$
>
> Let P be a source of light moving once around the ellipse
>
> $$\frac{x^2}{a^2} + \frac{y^2}{b^2} = 1$$
>
> in the $z = c + 1$ plane. Sketch and calculate the area of the shadow projected by R on the xy-plane.

Only the examinations from Germany reflected applications to business. These applications tended to deal with quality control and applications of probability to production problems. For example, the 1992 *abitur* (an examination given college-bound students) in the state of Bavaria contained the following item (Dossey, 1996):

> It is given that 8% of the golf balls made by a particular manufacturer are considered unusable by golf players. From past experience, it has been shown that 5% of the golf balls delivered by the manufacturer are returned because of defects. For every returned ball, the manufacturer takes a loss of 0.80 DM (*Deutsche Marks*), and for every ball not returned the manufacturer will make a net profit of 1.20 DM. What is the probability that the manufacturer will make a net profit of at least 210 DM on a 200-ball delivery?

One should be careful about criticizing the focus of most school-leaving examinations on applications of mathematics to classical problems in physics.

These problems remain valuable for many students who need the ability to translate and formulate problems drawing on the common languages of mathematics and science. These skills are inherently important for students continuing with the study of physics, engineering, and advanced mathematics.

Through a much broader and potentially richer set of mathematical activities for motivating a more diverse set of students, we can show *all* students the power of mathematics to effect change through decision-making in settings close to their lives. The ability to balance such traditional and contemporary forces in both curriculum and assessment will remain a challenge for years to come.

A U.S. View for All Students

The 1992 National Assessment of Educational Progress (NAEP) mathematics assessment evaluated the performance of a random sample of U.S. twelfth graders on a mixed set of tasks (Dossey, Mullis, & Jones, 1993). One task was somewhat similar to, but much simpler than, the motion problem given in the University of Tokyo examination:

> The darkened segments in the figure on the left below [Figure 9-1] show the path of an object that starts at point A and moves to point C at a constant rate of 1 unit per second. The object's distance from point A (or from point C) is the *shortest* distance between the object and the point. In the graph paper on the right, complete the following steps:
>
> **a.** Sketch the graph of the distance of the object from point A over the 7-second period.
>
> **b.** Then sketch the graph of the distance of the object from the point C over the same period.
>
> **c.** On your graph, label point P at the point where the distance of the object from point A is equal to the distance of the object from point C.
>
> **d.** Between which two consecutive seconds is the object equidistant from points A and C?

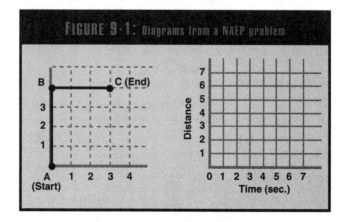

FIGURE 9-1: Diagrams from a NAEP problem

A second NAEP problem, set in perhaps a more real-world setting, asked students to consider the following situation involving a proposed income tax:

> One plan for a state income tax requires those persons with income of $10,000 or less to pay no tax and those persons with income greater than $10,000 to pay a tax of 6 percent only on the part of their income that exceeds $10,000.

> A person's *effective* tax rate is defined as the percent of total income that is paid in tax. Based on this definition, could any person's effective tax rate be 5 percent? Could it be 6 percent? Explain your answer. Include examples if necessary to justify your conclusion.

Students' performances on these two tasks were evaluated using a 6-point partial-credit rubric according to the categories of no response, totally incorrect work, minimal work, partial work, satisfactory work, and extended correct work. Only 1% of U.S. twelfth graders achieved one of the top two scoring categories (satisfactory or extended credit) for the particle-motion task. The performance was not much better for the tax item, where only 3% rated a satisfactory or extended score. These data are based on the performances of a random sample of U.S. students still attending school at the twelfth-grade level. The performance percentages would undoubtedly be lower if all youth of that age cohort were sampled.

SUMMARY

Contextualized extended-response items like those shown from NAEP are very demanding for U.S. students. However, they in no way reach the level of complexity expected of students of similar ages in the terminal year of secondary school mathematics in countries that are our economic peers. The tasks in this volume push the envelope further for U.S. students by requiring that our students be able to draw on information from outside the traditional mathematics/science connection. However, additional focus must be given to communicating the expectation that U.S. students be able to deal with non-routine problems in contextualized settings. The ability of mathematics educators, curriculum specialists, and assessment directors to coordinate this forward movement will require a great deal of effort.

Comparisons with school-leaving examinations in other countries are always difficult to interpret (Gandal & Dossey, 1997). The NAEP examinations are designed to collect information on a random sample of American 12th graders, regardless of the secondary school mathematics they have taken. The University of Tokyo examination is an exceedingly challenging entrance examination given to select the best of the excellent students applying for entrance to that university. Regardless of that difference in purpose—status of the system versus selection of individuals—the data and analysis from comparisons of examinations (Britton & Raizen, 1996; Gandal & Dossey, 1997) suggest that contextualized, non-routine tasks are not commonly included even on the mathematics examinations in other countries, although a great deal has been written concerning the need for such tasks. The U.S. experience with NAEP tasks requiring such work shows that students will need a great deal of support in formulating, solving, and communicating their results.

These cautions notwithstanding, the broad applications of mathematics in daily life, the need to motivate and retain students in mathematics, and the importance of reporting the ability levels of students in mathematics relative to the demands of the world all require that we begin to move both instruction and assessment to include tasks such as those illustrated in this volume. To do less is to abandon significant opportunities to relate the real world to the classroom while strengthening student problem-solving and modeling skills. The trick will be to balance this instruction and assessment with the concepts and skills that define the traditional core of mathematics. This is the real-life problem confronting the classroom teacher and the curriculum specialist.

REFERENCES

Britton, E. D. & Raizen, S. A. (Eds.). (1996). *Examining the examinations*. Boston, MA: Kluwer Academic Publishers.

Dossey, J. A. (1996). Mathematics examinations. In E. D. Britton & S. A. Raizen (Eds.), *Examining the examinations*, (pp. 165-195). Boston, MA: Kluwer Academic Publishers.

Dossey, J. A., Mullis, I. V. S., & Jones, C. (1993). *Can students do mathematical problem solving*. Washington, DC: National Center for Education Statistics.

Gandal, M. & Dossey, J. (1997). *What students abroad are expected to know about mathematics: Exams from France, Germany and Japan*. Washington, DC: American Federation of Teachers.

Wu, L. E. (1993). *Japanese university entrance examination problems in mathematics*. Washington, DC: Mathematical Association of America.

JOHN DOSSEY is the Distinguished University Professor of Mathematics at Illinois State University. He is Chair of the Conference Board of the Mathematical Sciences and has served as President of the National Council of Teachers of Mathematics, and as Chair of the U.S. National Commission on Mathematics Instruction at the National Research Council.

DRUG DOSAGE

TASK. A student strained her knee in an intramural volleyball game, and her doctor has prescribed an anti-inflammatory drug to reduce the swelling. She is to take two 220-milligram tablets every 8 hours for 10 days. Her kidneys filter 60% of this drug from her body every 8 hours. How much of the drug is in her system after 24 hours?

COMMENTARY. This task can be approached in many different ways using numeric or algebraic methods, by hand, with calculators or with computers. Regardless of their approach, mathematically literate students will need to be familiar with the mathematical structure in this task. Whether the situation involves understanding effective drug dosages, population growth, bank accounts or loans, amortization, heating or cooling, filtering pollution from lakes and streams, models of learning and forgetting, or models of the economy, students should be familiar with some of the many situations which give rise to *iterative processes*—repeated processes in which future levels are determined by present levels. The importance of technology in dealing with tasks of this type is worth noting. Students should be able to think and work with iterative processes, and also should be sufficiently comfortable with technology to expect, as a matter of course, to consider long-term behavior and trends. All high school graduates need to be comfortable with both the structure of such tasks and the technological tools for their investigation.

Iterative models illustrate a mathematical tool that has become increasingly important in recent years: difference equations, the discrete-time analogs of differential equations. In the past, students did not study difference equations until well into their undergraduate or graduate courses. But with the aid of a spreadsheet or graphing calculator, students can handle such iterative problems with relative ease, provided that they can make the translation from a problem statement to an equation describing the iterative process, also called a *recursion equation*.

MATHEMATICAL ANALYSIS. One approach is to create a table of values relating the number of 8-hour periods to the amount of the drug remaining in the student's system. To do this, some assumptions must be made about how quickly the drug gets into her system after it is taken. The simplest model assumes that the drug is active immediately after the medication is taken.

In this task, the information given is the rate at which the drug is eliminated by the kidney, whereas the focus of the tasks is on how much remains. The fundamental unit of time is an 8-hour period.

If the student takes 440 mg of the anti-inflammatory drug, after 8 hours her kidneys have removed 60% of the 440 mg, leaving 40% of the dose in her system. After she has taken her second 440-mg dose, the total amount of drug in her system in mg is then: $(.4)(440) + 440 = 616$. After 16 hours, she has 40% of the total for 8 hours, plus another 440. After 24 hours, she has 40% of the total for 16 hours, plus another 440. These calculations are summarized in Table 1.

One way to generalize this method is to use Table 1 to see patterns. First, let A_n denote the amount of drug in the system after dose n. Then the "drug remaining" column may be represented as in Table 2. The relationship in Table 2 between the "drug remaining" column and the "total in system" column may then be represented as shown in Table 3, which can easily be converted into a spreadsheet. Table 3 also suggests the recursion equation: $.4A_{n-1} + 440 = A_n$, where A_n is the amount of drug present at the beginning of the nth 8-hour period (or nth dose).

More advanced students might begin their solutions by modeling the process with this recursion equation, expressing the relationship between A_{n-1} and A_n. Such an equation is well suited for use in a programmable calculator or a spreadsheet, especially in investigating the long-term behavior of the model.

TABLE 1: Calculation of amount of drug in system						
DAY	TIME IN HOURS	DRUG REMAINING	+	AMOUNT TAKEN	=	TOTAL IN SYSTEM
1	0	0	+	440	=	440
1	8	176	+	440	=	616
1	16	246.40	+	440	=	686.4
2	24	274.56	+	440	=	714.56

TABLE 2: Calculation of amount of drug in system, first generalization					
DOSE n	DRUG REMAINING	+	AMOUNT TAKEN	=	TOTAL IN SYSTEM, A_n
1	0	+	440	=	440 A_1
2	(.4)(440)	+	440	=	616 A_2
3	(.4)(616)	+	440	=	686.4 A_3
4	(.4)(686.4)	+	440	=	714.56 A_4

TABLE 3: Calculation of amount of drug in system, second generalization					
DOSE n	DRUG REMAINING	+	AMOUNT TAKEN	=	TOTAL IN SYSTEM, A_n
1	0	+	440	=	A1
2	(.4)A1	+	440	=	A2
3	(.4)A2	+	440	=	A3
4	(.4)A3	+	440	=	A4

Students who have studied iterative models may also solve this equation analytically to find an explicit formula for A_n.

EXTENSIONS. How much of the drug is in the student's system after 10 days? The recursion equation above can be translated into a spreadsheet to answer this. Students will notice that the peak levels, A_n, don't get bigger indefinitely and can investigate ways of determining the limiting value.

Suppose she doesn't like taking medicine, so she decides to take only one pill every 8 hours for 20 days. Does this strategy of taking half the amount of the drug for twice as long a period result in the same level of drug in her system? Many drugs have what is known as a therapeutic level. Unless the amount of drug in one's system reaches the therapeutic level, the drug is not effective. If the therapeutic level for the drug she is taking is 650 mg, how effective is her strategy of taking half the drug for twice as long?

Sometimes doctors suggest that the patient take a double dose initially, called a loading dose. A simple variation in the standard model can illustrate the effect of the loading dose on the effectiveness of the drug.

In addition to a therapeutic level, drugs also have a toxic level. If too much of the drug is in your system, you can become ill as a result. As you age, the ability of your kidneys and liver to remove the drug is reduced. Suppose that, for older patients, only 40% of the drug is removed in an 8-hour period. What dangers does this pose for older patients? How would such a patient fare using a strategy of taking only one tablet for twice as long?

Once these situations have been examined, students could explore different dosages (e.g., two 200-milligram pills); dosage intervals, (e.g., taking one 220-milligram pill every 4 hours); and clearing rates (for example, the kidneys of most healthy individuals will filter 45% to 65% of the drug from their system within 8 hours). Though it requires more sophisticated methods for solution, students could also explore different models in which the drug does not get into the bloodstream immediately.

Some medications, particularly cold capsules, contain several different drugs. The liver and kidneys remove nearly 70% of a typical decongestant in an 8-hour period but only approximately 20% of a typical antihistamine during the same period. If a student takes one decongestant and one antihistamine every 8 hours for 5 days, how does the level of decongestant compare to the level of antihistamine? Once the initial spreadsheet or calculator formulas are created, this very sophisticated question is within reach.

Often the information on the rate of filtering by the liver and kidneys is given in terms of the half-life of the drug. For example, theophylline, a common asthma drug, has a half-life of approximately 4 hours. Local pharmacists can identify the half-life of drugs that people typically take during cold and flu season. Students can rewrite the half-life of the drugs in terms of the decay rate for the interval of time between doses of the medication. Since half-life is such a commonly given measure, it is important that students be able to use this terminology as well to compare residual levels over specific time periods.

MENTAL MATHEMATICS

TASKS

1. In a 6th grade mathematics class, one of the problems requires the following calculation: $\frac{15}{32} \div \frac{3}{8}$. One student claims, without using pencil or paper, that the answer is $\frac{5}{4}$ because $15 \div 3 = 5$ and $32 \div 8 = 4$. Is the student's answer correct? How can the student's reasoning be explained?

2. The owners of a manufacturing company would like to be able to promise one-week delivery of special orders. The company is not ready, however, to make this promise to customers. Of the 56 orders filled so far this month, 49 were filled in one week or less and 7 took more than one week to fill, a success rate of 87.5%. During the weekly team meeting, the supervisor wants to know how many subsequent orders must be filled within one week to increase this month's success rate to 90%. Several employees know that this problem can be solved with algebra and scrounge around for paper and pencils. One employee, however, announces that the answer is 14. She describes her reasoning as follows: We want the 7 late orders so far to be only 10% of the total number of orders, which therefore must be 70. Subtracting the 49 on-time and 7 late orders so far yields 14 orders. Is she correct? How can her reasoning be explained?

COMMENTARY. Mental arithmetic can save time, money, and even embarrassment—such as being caught short of cash at the check-out counter. In everyday life, people use mental arithmetic to estimate budgets, shopping bills, tips in restaurants, and taxes. On the job, an employee might be asked to give a quick estimate while talking to a boss or a colleague. Mental arithmetic depends not only upon number facts and estimating skills but also problem solving skills and algebraic reasoning skills because the standard paper-and-pencil algorithms are sometimes hard to do in one's head. As people become more familiar with number facts and gain number sense and symbol sense, their mental arithmetic can become more precise and more flexible. A study of 44 mathematicians' numerical estimation strategies found considerable variation in the strategies used (Dowker, 1992). As many as 23 different strategies were used for the same task!

The value in discussing mental arithmetic in high school is that number sense and symbol sense can build on each other, leading to greater facility with and understanding of both algebra and mental arithmetic. The examples above have been chosen to illustrate this possibility. In beginning algebra classes, students often arrive at answers without using symbolic techniques. Furthermore, as these examples illustrate, informal or non-standard methods can reveal sophisticated algebraic reasoning, even though it might not be expressed symbolically. Rather than disregarding such informal methods as distractions from the goal of teaching standard algebraic methods, teachers can exploit informal methods as sources of meaning for students by establishing connections between informal and formal methods. Such connections can go in two directions. First, an informal method may be expressed symbolically, thereby promoting algebra as a way of expressing ideas about numbers. In this way, symbol sense may build upon number sense. Second, after some manipulation, symbolic expressions may be reinterpreted informally, thereby promoting algebra as a way of thinking about numbers. In this way, number sense may build upon symbol sense.

For experienced users of algebra, some of its power of comes from the fact that symbols may be manipulated without concern for their meaning. Nevertheless, for students and experienced users alike, periodic re-interpretation of symbolic expressions can shed new light on the context, its mathematical representations, or its mathematical structure, potentially leading toward an understanding of algebra that is more flexible for solving familiar and unfamiliar problems.

MATHEMATICAL ANALYSIS. Each task is solved separately below.

1. It is easy to verify that the student's answer is indeed correct:

$$\frac{15}{32} \div \frac{3}{8} = \frac{15}{32} \cdot \frac{8}{3} = \frac{5 \cdot 3}{8 \cdot 4} \cdot \frac{8}{3} = \frac{5}{4}$$

But the calculation does not shed much light on whether the approach makes sense. One way of explaining the approach is to note that if the calculation were $\frac{15}{32} \div \frac{3}{32}$, the answer would be 5, because 15 of anything divided by 3 of the same things is 5. But because we are dividing by $\frac{3}{8}$, which is 4 times bigger than $\frac{3}{32}$, the answer should be $\frac{1}{4}$ of 5, or $\frac{5}{4}$.

Another way to justify the approach is algebraic. The standard method is as follows:

$$\frac{a}{b} \div \frac{c}{d} = \frac{a}{b} \cdot \frac{d}{c} = \frac{ad}{bc}$$

The student proposes that the answer is $\frac{a \div c}{b \div d}$. Simplifying this expression according to standard algebraic rules shows that the answer is indeed correct:

$$\frac{a \div c}{b \div d} = \frac{\frac{a}{c}}{\frac{b}{d}} = \frac{a}{c} \div \frac{b}{d} = \frac{a}{c} \cdot \frac{d}{b} = \frac{ad}{bc}$$

The awkwardness of the calculation, however, suggests that this approach, although correct, might not be efficient if, for example, c is not a factor of a.

2. Other employees might check the employee's answer. With 49 successes and 7 failures so far, and 14 future successes, the success rate will be:

$$\frac{49 + 14}{49 + 7 + 14} = \frac{63}{70} = 0.90, \text{ or } 90\%.$$

So her answer is correct. The deeper question is how to explain the employee's reasoning. Her reasoning is clear and understandable, too, indicating that there is probably a general procedure at work. What, then, is the relationship between her reasoning and the standard algebraic approach?

A typical way to solve the problem that the supervisor poses would be to let x represent the unknown number of subsequent (consecutive) orders to be delivered successfully within one week. Then,

$$\frac{49 + x}{49 + 7 + x} = 0.90$$

But this equation is hard to solve mentally. To generalize this approach, let x be as above, let r represent the desired success rate, let s represent the number of successes so far, and let f represent the number failures so far. Then, as before,

$$\frac{s + x}{s + f + x} = r \qquad \textbf{(1)}$$

Solving this for *x* yields (after some manipulation):

$$x = \frac{rs + rf - s}{1 - r} \qquad (2)$$

Though it is not immediately clear how to interpret this formula, the denominator, $1 - r$, gives a clue about the employee's reasoning: if *r* is the desired success rate, then $1 - r$ is the desired failure rate, and the employee's reasoning began with the failure rate —10% in this case. Equation 1, which is based on successes, has an analog that is based on failures. Table 1 gives the analogous equation and several others that follow algebraically from it, along with explanations of how the equation might be interpreted.

The last equation in Table 1 is close to the reasoning that the employee described, and is a general procedure that may be done mentally. Thus, algebraic manipulation has provided justification for the employee's mental procedure.

Algebra can also provide suggestions for other mental procedures. Further algebraic manipulation of Equation 2, for example, gives additional possibilities, shown in Table 2.

TABLE 1: Equations relating successes and failures, with interpretations	
EQUATION	INTERPRETATION
$\frac{f}{s + f + x} = 1 - r$	The failure rate, the number of failures over the total number of orders this month (past and future), is equal to 1 minus the success rate.
$\frac{f}{1 - r} = s + f + x$	Dividing the number of failures by the target failure rate gives the total number of orders required.
$x = \frac{f}{1 - r} - s - f$	The number of consecutive new successes required can be calculated as follows: Divide the number of failures by the target failure rate (yielding the total number of orders required), and subtract the number of orders so far (both successes and failures).

TABLE 2: More equations relating successes and failures, with interpretations	
EQUATION	INTERPRETATION
$\frac{s + x}{r} = \frac{f}{1 - r}$	The number of successes (both past and future) is to the success rate as the number of failures is to the failure rate.
$\frac{s + x}{f} = \frac{r}{1 - r}$	The ratio of successes to failures must be the same as the ratio of the success rate to the failure rate.

The last equation in Table 2 gives another way to think about the original problem. Because the ratio of the desired success rate and failure rate is 90:10 or 9:1, there must be 9 times as many successes as failures. With 7 failures so far, there must be 63 successes, or 14 more than the 49 we already have.

EXTENSIONS. Traditional algebra problems can present similar opportunities for students to generate informal solutions. For example,

$$\text{Box} + \text{Box} + \text{Box} + \text{Triangle} = 47$$
$$\text{Box} - \text{Triangle} = 1$$

A student might say, "Well, I know from the second equation that Box is one more than Triangle. So I imagined that the Triangle in the first equation was a Box. Then the first equation would be Box + Box + Box + Box = 48. So, Box is 12 and Triangle is 11."

REFERENCES

Dowker, A. (1992). Computational estimation strategies of professional mathematicians. *Journal for Research in Mathematics Education, 23*(1), 45-55.

BUYING ON CREDIT

TASK. A credit card company, whose motto is "see the world on credit," charges 1.387% interest on the unpaid balance in an account each month, and requires a minimum payment of 2% of the outstanding balance each month. Suppose you charge $100 each month and make only the minimum payment each month. How much will you owe at the time of your 24th bill? Assuming you pay the whole bill at the end of that period, how much will be interest?

COMMENTARY. Consumer debt is a big issue in this country. Thanks to the widespread availability of calculators and computers, consumers can easily do the calculations themselves to better understand the cost of maintaining credit card balances.

Powerful tools for this job are spreadsheets and programmable and graphing calculators. Mathematical analysis is still necessary, of course, but technology provides an avenue for mathematical modeling that gives students straightforward access to some mathematics that once required much more background. Once the spreadsheet is set up, students can explore different payment options and see the consequences. Spreadsheets can help demystify mathematics and provide an exploratory medium for doing calculations that are both relevant and meaningful for students.

MATHEMATICAL ANALYSIS. The general mathematical structure of this task is the same as that of **Drug Dosage** (p. 80), and solutions can be obtained in similar ways. To analyze what happens when making only the minimum monthly payment, one might start with a table in order to obtain a recursion equation. That equation can be solved or used in a calculator or a spreadsheet.

In addition to charging interest on the previous month's unpaid balance, most credit card companies charge interest on new purchases, too, when the customer is carrying a balance. (The typical 25-day, interest-free grace period applies only if the entire balance is paid off each month.) The interest is usually computed based on an "average daily balance," so the actual amount of interest depends upon when the payment arrives and when the new charge is made. To simplify the calculations, assume that both the new charge and the payment come in at the end of the billing cycle and do not affect the interest that month.

To obtain a recursion equation, let x_n be the amount of the nth statement. Because the minimum payment is 2% of x_n, then, each month,

- the amount of the payment is $.02x_n$,
- the interest charge is $.01387x_n$, and
- there is an additional $100 of purchases.

So to find x_{n+1} (the amount of the $(n + 1)$st statement), the payment is subtracted from and the other amounts are added to x_n, the amount of the nth statement:

$$x_{n+1} = x_n - .02x_n + .01387x_n + 100$$

or

$$x_{n+1} = .99387x_n + 100.$$

To find out how much will be owed at the time of the 24th bill, start with $x_1 = 100$, and repeat the calculation 23 times. Or, with a programmable calculator, define $x_1 = 100$ and x_{n+1} by the formula given above and tell the program to calculate x_{24}.

To calculate using a spreadsheet, begin with the first row which probably has cells named as shown in Table 1. In a spreadsheet, these cells might be used to contain the information shown in Table 2.

In the first month, there is no previous bill, no minimum payment, no unpaid balance, and no interest. Enter 100 in cell D1 representing the new charges and 100 in E1 to represent the balance at the end of month 1.

In the second row, enter the numbers and formulas shown in Table 3. Then formulas for the next 22 rows are the same, except that the row numbers will change. Most spreadsheet programs will change the row numbers automatically if these cells are copied and then pasted into the next 22 rows. The spreadsheet will create a table similar to Table 4.

The spreadsheet can total the columns, too, as illustrated. Table 4 shows that if you pay in the way suggested, you will have made $527.97 in payments on your $2,400 in purchases and still owe $2,238.18 because of $366.14 in interest.

If the calculations in Table 4 are correct, the purchases plus the interest minus the payments should give the outstanding balance.

Purchases + Interest − Payments =
$2,400 + $366.14 − $527.97 = $2,238.17

so the calculations are off by a penny somewhere. By asking the spreadsheet to display its results more accurately, it becomes clear that there is not a mistake, just "round-off" error.

TABLE 1: Names of cells in a spreadsheet				
A1	B1	C1	D1	E1

TABLE 2: How data might be organized in a spreadsheet				
The previous bill	The minimum payment	The interest	The new charges	The new balance

TABLE 3: Formulas for one row of the spreadsheet[1]				
E1	.02*A2	.01387*A2	$100	A2−B2+C2+D2

MONTH	PREVIOUS BALANCE	PAYMENT	INTEREST	PURCHASES	NEW BALANCE
	A	B	C	D	E
1				$100.00	$100.00
2	$100.00	$2.00	$1.39	$100.00	$199.39
3	$199.39	$3.99	$2.77	$100.00	$298.16
4	$298.16	$5.96	$4.14	$100.00	$396.34
5	$396.34	$7.93	$5.50	$100.00	$493.91
6	$493.91	$9.88	$6.85	$100.00	$590.88
7	$590.88	$11.82	$8.20	$100.00	$687.26
8	$687.26	$13.75	$9.53	$100.00	$783.04
9	$783.04	$15.66	$10.86	$100.00	$878.24
10	$878.24	$17.56	$12.18	$100.00	$972.86
11	$972.86	$19.46	$13.49	$100.00	$1,066.90
12	$1,066.90	$21.34	$14.80	$100.00	$1,160.36
13	$1,160.36	$23.21	$16.09	$100.00	$1,253.24
14	$1,253.24	$25.06	$17.38	$100.00	$1,345.56
15	$1,345.56	$26.91	$18.66	$100.00	$1,437.31
16	$1,437.31	$28.75	$19.94	$100.00	$1,528.50
17	$1,528.50	$30.57	$21.20	$100.00	$1,619.13
18	$1,619.13	$32.38	$22.46	$100.00	$1,709.21
19	$1,709.21	$34.18	$23.71	$100.00	$1,798.73
20	$1,798.73	$35.97	$24.95	$100.00	$1,887.70
21	$1,887.70	$37.75	$26.18	$100.00	$1,976.13
22	$1,976.13	$39.52	$27.41	$100.00	$2,064.02
23	$2,064.02	$41.28	$28.63	$100.00	$2,151.37
24	$2,151.37	$43.03	$29.84	$100.00	$2,238.18
TOTAL		$527.97	$366.14	$2,400.00	

TABLE 4: The completed spreadsheet[2]

Purchases + Interest – Payments =
$2,400 + $366.1438 – $527.9651 = $2,231.1787.

See **Rounding Off** (p. 119) for further discussion of this issue.

EXTENSIONS. The solution above made several assumptions to simplify the calculations. Some extensions can bring the solution closer to the way the credit card companies actually do their computations:

• For which of the above calculations is rounding necessary? Fix the table in the spreadsheet to properly account for rounding.

• For many credit card companies, the minimum payment is always a whole-dollar amount. Incorporate this idea into the solution.

• Expand on the solution above so that the dates of payments and new charges could be varied and so that the interest would be calculated according to an average daily balance. Investigate how the dates of payments and new charges affect the interest charges.

Other extensions could investigate alternative scenarios. Suppose, for example, you spent $2,400 up front and then made the minimum payment for each of 24 months. What would the accrued interest be?

The commentary mentioned that the mathematical structure of this task is the same as that of **Drug Dosage** (p. 80). **Lottery Winnings** (p. 111) also shares the same basic structure. Once students have sufficient experience with tasks like these, they might explore the difference and similarities among the procedures, formulas, and solutions of these tasks.

NOTES

1. Here, as in many spreadsheet programs, an asterisk serves as a multiplication sign. In some spreadsheet programs, formulas must be preceded with an equals sign, so that, for example, the contents of the second cell would instead be: =.02*A1.
2. The column headings are provided for clarity, but are not part of the spreadsheet. Conveniently, the row numbers can function as month numbers.

PART THREE

CURRICULAR CONSIDERATIONS

OVERVIEW

ny discussion of curriculum assumes, whether implicitly or explicitly, one of many views of curriculum. College admissions requirements, for example, sometimes describe a high school mathematics curriculum as little more than a list of course titles. Toward the other end of specificity, some might point to a textbook, looking especially at its table of contents. For the purposes of this document, a *curriculum* is a detailed plan for instruction, including not only the materials used by teachers and students, but also understandings of how they fit together and of the important mathematical concepts embedded within them. Thus, a mathematics curriculum might include—*but must not be limited to*—tasks such as those in this volume. The essays in Part Three in particular go beyond a list of topics, beyond a collection of tasks, to discuss how curricula might be constructed—how tasks, topics, and "habits of mind" might be knit together as themes or strands to create a curriculum with coherence, depth, and rich opportunity for student learning, sense making, and connections to students' ways of thinking about the world.

In his essay, Zalman Usiskin discusses the importance of applying knowledge to new situations. When designing curriculum, he begins with a key concept and seeks models—settings, often from the workplace or everyday life, which embody the mathematical ideas. Of course, for many users of mathematics, it is more common to go in the other direction—to begin with a real-world setting and seek a mathematical model of that setting, perhaps with graphs or formulas. Chazan and Bethell (p. 35) describe such an approach earlier in this volume. They put students into the workplace and asked them to find the mathematics. Thus, whether the mathematics models the world or the world models the mathematics depends upon where you begin. Ultimately, both directions might be necessary for students to make strong connections between mathematics and their worlds. In discussing the role of tasks in curriculum, Usiskin suggests organizing curriculum around sequences of such models and problems that range over many years.

Albert Cuoco takes another approach to organizing curriculum. He suggests that mathematics is more than a collection of topics organized under broad headings such as geometry and number but, rather, is about ways of thinking, or *habits of mind*, such as algorithmic thinking, proportional reasoning, and reasoning through thought experiment. Habits of mind, he suggests, can be threads that help organize curriculum, for without habits of mind, higher order skills will remain elusive.

Harvey Keynes' essay discusses a key theme in this document: effectively preparing students for work and for higher education. Keynes asks two important questions: First, what are characteristics of tasks that can prepare students both for the workplace and for postsecondary education? Second, what are the requirements for effective use of tasks like these in the classroom? Keynes suggests conditions of appropriateness for tasks that can develop both concrete and abstract thinking.

The tasks in Part Three differ from those in other parts to illustrate that they may be fruitfully approached at many different times in a student's mathematical career. The discussions of these tasks include multiple solutions, many extensions, and more connections to other mathematical ways of thinking. Some of this discussion is quite deep mathematically, not to suggest that such depth is appropriate for all students at the same time, but, rather, to suggest that these tasks can provide opportunity for engagement in rich and deep mathematics to students when they are interested and ready. Tasks that are sufficiently rich and that satisfy Keynes' conditions for appropriateness can fit more than once into a curriculum that is organized around Cuoco's "habits of mind" or Usiskin's sequences of models.

The **Lottery Winnings** (p. 111) task may be solved at one level with spreadsheets, for students having little formal algebraic experience, and it may be used to motivate students to see a need for the general symbolic language that algebra provides. At another level, students who are more experienced with the symbolism of algebra might be expected to express the task's spreadsheet relationships in standard algebraic notation. Students with even more sophistication might be expected to find the general formula. In a pre-calculus course, students might explore these lottery winnings with annual, semi-annual, monthly, weekly, and daily payments as excellent background for the important calculus idea of successive approximation.

The other tasks in this part are similarly rich. In addition to discussion of probability and Simpson's paradox, **Hospital Quality** (p. 115) can lead to exploration of ideas about rates, ordered pairs, and vectors. **Rounding Off** (p. 119) provides opportunities for exploring ideas in algebra and arithmetic, while serving as an introduction to the idea of using geometry to represent probability. **Rules of Thumb** (p. 123) can lead to discussion of modeling and comparison of linear models, or linear and quadratic models. The many avenues of approach to these tasks may be exploited by teachers to maximize connections to students' thinking and experience.

The idea of periodically revisiting tasks sounds rather like Bruner's spiral curriculum (Bruner, 1965/1960), an idea that some might argue has lost its usefulness. Data from the Third International Mathematics and Science Study (TIMSS) (Schmidt, McKnight, & Raizen, 1996) suggest, however, that there has been a degeneration of the spiral curriculum as Bruner saw it. The point of Bruner's spiral curriculum was not that topics should be repeated for several years until they "stick" but that, when an idea is revisited in a new setting or with new tools, if students have opportunity to connect the new encounter to their understandings of their previous encounters with the idea (along with all the intervening experiences), then their understanding can grow.

There are dangers in any statements of standards or suggested visions of school mathematics, for there is no clear path indicating what should happen in classrooms. Cuoco warns that the statement, "Students should be able to solve problems like these," can become "Students should be able to solve these problems." But such a conclusion is contrary to the intention of this volume. The goals are for students to learn mathematics and to learn to appreciate the power that mathematics holds for us. Any task or collection of tasks is merely intended to be a means to those ends. Furthermore, teaching any task as only a procedure to be memorized will destroy its richness. Our point—especially in evoking the image of the spiral curriculum— is that there is value in revisiting tasks such as these at various points in a student's career, each time aiming for more sophisticated analysis and deeper mathematics.

In summary, the tasks in this volume cannot comprise a high school mathematics curriculum; no small collection of tasks could. These tasks have been chosen for their illustrative richness rather than for any collective curricular coherence. Individually and collectively, these tasks together with the essays might instead serve as inspiration for those interested in curriculum, but, as curriculum designers know, there is a lot of work to be done between first noting that there is mathematics in some real-world context and finally developing good curricular materials.

REFERENCES

Bruner, J. S. (1965/1960). *The process of education*. Cambridge, MA: Harvard University Press.

Schmidt, W. H., McKnight, C. C., & Raizen, S. A. (1996). *A splintered vision: An investigation of U.S. science and mathematics education*. Dordrecht, The Netherlands: Kluwer Academic Publishers.

10 FITTING TASKS TO CURRICULUM

ZALMAN USISKIN
UNIVERSITY OF CHICAGO

When I first taught high school, I used to tell my students—even the average ones—that the real test of learning was not whether they could answer questions like those they had seen in their textbooks but whether they could apply their knowledge to new situations they had not encountered. This aphorism is only partially true and was patently unfair. In applying the principle of the aphorism, when I would make up a test, I would purposely choose items that students had not encountered, items for which they would not have studied. Those items were not a test of what had been learned from the class but what had *not* been learned from the class. They tested some natural or acquired competence beyond the course.

Those who wish students to apply, synthesize, analyze, and evaluate (to use the language of higher mental processes found in Bloom's *Taxonomy of Educational Objectives* [1956]) have always found it difficult to invent representative items. Those for whom a problem is "a situation which we want to resolve but for which we do not have an algorithm" (to use the common researcher definition) have a similar dilemma, for once a problem is solved, the astute solver has an algorithm to use for the next problem of that type. Inventing good problems has always been an art.

The quandary presented by the desire to have students *apply* their knowledge and not just parrot it has been felt by all those whose goals involve more than routine skills. In the 1970's, when in a reaction to one of the weaknesses of the "new math" we began to design curricula in which a main goal was to have students apply what they knew in real-world situations, the same dilemma appeared in only slightly different clothing. We felt strongly that students were not able to apply algebra because they were not taught the applications. But if we taught the applications, then were we not changing "application" from a higher level process to a lower one?

We decided that the goal of learning to apply was more important than how that learning had been attained; that is, we decided to teach the applications. For example, consider the following problem, introduced in *Algebra Through Applications with Probability and Statistics* (Usiskin, 1979).

> In Chicago there are two monthly rates for local telephone service. Choice 1 has a base rate of $11.25 for 200 calls plus .0523 for each call over 200. Choice 2 is $24.50 for an unlimited number of calls. How do you decide which plan is better?

Students were asked to write a sentence that would help them decide. The goal was to think of the sentence $11.25 + .0523(x - 200) > 24.5$ (When is choice 1 better?) or $11.25 + .0523(x - 200) < 24.5$ (When is choice 2 better?). This is not an easy task for students who have never studied problems like these. But we wanted to make solving such problems routine because they abound in the real world. The lesson contained similar items involving teacher salaries (compare $9,000 plus $500 for each year's experience with $9,750 plus $350 for each year) and rental cars (compare $15.95 a day plus 14¢ a mile with $12.95 a day plus 15¢ a mile). Fitting the title of the lesson, "Decision-Making Using Sentences," students were not asked to solve the sentences they wrote. The problems were employed to motivate the *next* lesson, in which students were shown an algorithm for solving $ax + b \leq cx + d$, and were given additional problems of the type.

"Problems of the type" is an important phrase to consider. What type is involved here? A current view is that it is unwise to sort problems by their context, such as has been the tradition in algebra with coin problems, mixture problems, distance-rate-time problems, age problems, and so on. Yet, on the other hand, Polya's advice is also commonly accepted: "If you cannot solve the proposed problem try to solve first some related problem" (Polya, 1957). When is a problem to be considered as "related"? How should we group problems for study?

The consequences of grouping related problems reach far beyond explication of types. With respect to problem solving, the power of mathematics lies in its ability to solve entire classes of problems with similar techniques. The Chicago telephone-cost problem is not an earth-shaking context for mathematics, but it exemplifies a class of *constant increase* problems that lead to equations and functions involving the algebraic form $ax + b$. Put another way, if we expect students to come up with a mathematical model for a real situation, they need to know the attributes of the situation that would cause a particular mathematical model (linear, quadratic, exponential, sine wave, etc.) to be appropriate.

So, in developing the University of Chicago School Mathematics Project curricula that give strong attention to applications, we have often begun with the mathematical concept and sought the key mathematical models of that concept (University of Chicago School Mathematics Project, 1989-97; Usiskin, 1991). In a few instances, the content is standard in the curriculum, as with growth and decay models for exponential functions. In other cases, the mathematical conceptualizations of the topic need to be broadened; as with angle, for example, which in geometry is traditionally "the union of two rays," but which in applications may be better conceptualized as a "turn" or as a "difference in directions." Freudenthal (1983) has done many analyses of this kind.

In a few cases, we have found that the standard approach to the problem type to be inhibiting. Consider the following problem, which originates from an actual situation:

> A city charges 8% tax and a restaurant in the city gives a 5% discount for paying cash. Is it better for a diner if the discount is given first and the tax charged on the discounted price, or if the tax is charged on the discounted price, and then the discount taken?

Students are customarily taught that taxes (discounts) are added to (subtracted from) original prices to determine total cost. Thinking this way, working from a meal with original cost M, the first option is represented by the expression

$$(M - .05M) + .08(M - .05M).$$

If, instead, students are taught to think of taxes and discounts as factors, i.e., to think multiplicatively, that same option is represented by $1.08(.95M)$. The multiplicative representation is not only simpler but makes transparent the desired generalization from doing this sort of problem: it makes no difference what the specific discounts and taxes are; if they are fixed they can be done in any order.

Fitting tasks to curriculum involves more than assuring that the *scope* of the curriculum is broad enough to accommodate the tasks. There is also the question of the *sequence* of topics. The mathematics you will see illustrated in the **Lottery Winnings** (p. 111) task involves the general idea of annuities, which can be viewed as the sums of compound interest expressions, which themselves trace back to the same multiplicative idea in the restaurant example given immediately above, which in turn requires that a student have the notion that multiplication by a number larger than 1 serves to enlarge a quantity, and multiplication by a number between 0 and 1 serves to contract it.

In the past, the mathematics curriculum has been carefully sequenced either by algorithmic considerations (to perform long division, you must be able to subtract and multiply, so these operations must precede division) or by logical considerations (one proof of the Pythagorean Theorem involves similar triangles, so these must be studied before the Pythagorean Theorem can be considered). The above analysis suggests that the development of problem-solving among the populace would be aided by the development of sequences of models and problems that range over many years of study.

Here is an example of such a development. Begin in the primary grades with the use of subtraction for *comparison* and the specific example of change. When division is introduced, cover the wide range of *rates* such as students/class, km/hr, and people/mi². In middle school, use negative numbers to represent measures in situations that have two opposing directions, such as gain and loss, up and down, or north and south, and picture them on the number line. Introduce ordered pairs, not only for cataloguing the locations of objects but also for recording pairs of data. Then, by asking how fast something has changed, introduce the concept of *rate of change*, picture this in the coordinate plane, and use both the application and the picture to lead into the idea of slope. In high school, study situations in which the rate of change is not constant. Use these to consider limits of rates of change. There is reasonable evidence that such an approach is far more effective in leading to understanding of the pure and applied mathematics involved than traditional approaches, in which the idea of slope is introduced by a definition as $(y_2 - y_1)/(x_2 - x_1)$ with no prior buildup or connection to rate of change.

Another example is geometric. In the elementary grades, use the familiar coordinate square grid to obtain areas of rectilinear figures and associate the product xy with the area of a rectangle with dimensions x and y. But also modify the square or rectangular grid to generate tessellations. Point out that a two-dimensional object that tessellates can be cut from a large sheet without wasting space. In the middle grades or early high school, use finer and finer grids to provide better and better estimates of the areas of regions. In high school, graph the speed of a car or other object over time, and interpret the area between the graph and the x-axis as the product of the speed and the time, i.e., as the distance traveled. This paves the way for the many situations representable with integrals.

It is significant that the long sequences described in the preceding two paragraphs are embedded in the traditional content of arithmetic, algebra, geometry, and elementary analysis. We have yet, however, to develop long sequences for the teaching of statistics, as it has had a shorter lifetime in the high school curriculum. To incorporate tasks like those in this volume into the experience of students is a curricular problem that is currently being undertaken by some of the mathematics reform curricula.

Even with the analysis of individual tasks and their setting in the curriculum, there remain two particularly knotty curricular problems. First, there are tasks that involve a range of mathematics too wide to be classified by a single mathematical model or even a family of related models. Incorporating these tasks into a curriculum is on the one hand easy because they can fit in so many places. On the other hand, without such a broader context in which to embed them, such tasks become unwieldy if students are not well versed in the prerequisites to them.

Second is the issue with which this essay began. While a fundamental goal of mathematics education must remain for students to acquire the competencies to solve simple and complex problems they are likely to encounter in their lives, students must also have opportunities to approach problems the likes of which they have not seen before. A task for curriculum developers is to accommodate these two competing needs. The corresponding task for philosophers and policy makers is to consider whether it is fair for everyday classroom assessments to test students on the latter.

REFERENCES

Bloom, B. (Ed.). (1956). *Taxonomy of educational objectives. Handbook I: Cognitive domain.* New York: David McKay.

Freudenthal, H. (1983). *Didactical phenomenology of mathematical structures.* Dordrecht, The Netherlands: Kluwer Academic Publishers.

Polya, G. (1957). *How to solve it.* (Second ed.). Princeton, NJ: Princeton University Press.

University of Chicago School Mathematics Project. (1989-97). *Transition mathematics. Algebra. Geometry. Advanced Algebra. Functions, statistics, and trigonometry.* Glenview, IL: Scott Foresman.

Usiskin, Z. (1979). *Algebra through applications with probability and statistics.* Reston, VA: National Council of Teachers of Mathematics.

Usiskin, Z. (1991). Building mathematics curricula with applications and modelling. In M. Niss, W. Blum, & I. Huntley (Eds.), *Teaching of mathematical modelling and applications*, (pp. 30-45). London: Ellis Horwood, Ltd.

ZALMAN USISKIN is Professor of Education at the University of Chicago and Director of the University of Chicago School Mathematics Project. He is a member of the Board of Directors of the National Council of Teachers of Mathematics, of the Mathematics/Science Standing Committee of the National Assessment of Educational Progress, and of the United States National Commission on Mathematical Instruction. He has served as a member of the Mathematical Sciences Education Board.

11 Mathematics as a Way of Thinking About Things

Albert A. Cuoco
Education Development Center

didn't always feel this way about mathematics. When I started teaching high school, I thought that mathematics was an ever-growing body of knowledge. Algebra was about equations, geometry was about space, arithmetic was about numbers; every branch of mathematics was about some particular mathematical objects. Gradually, I began to realize that what my students (some of them, anyway) were really taking away from my classes was a style of work that manifested itself between the lines in our discussions about triangles and polynomials and sample spaces. I began to see my discipline not only as a collection of results and conjectures but also as a collection of *habits of mind*.

This realization first became a conscious one for me when my family and I were building a house at the same time I was researching a problem in number theory. Now, pounding nails seems nothing like proving theorems, but I began to notice a remarkable similarity between the two projects. The similarity did not come from the fact that house-building requires applications of results from elementary mathematics (it does, by the way); rather, house-building and theorem-proving are alike, I realized, because of the kinds of thinking they require. Both require you to perform thought experiments, to visualize things that don't (yet) exist, to predict results of experiments that would be impossible to actually carry out, to tease out efficient algorithms from seemingly ad hoc actions, to deal with complexity, and to find similarities among seemingly different phenomena.

This focus on mathematical ways of thinking has been the emphasis in my classes and curriculum writing ever since, and I'm now convinced that, more than any specific result or skill, more than the Pythagorean Theorem or the fundamental theorem of algebra, these mathematical habits of mind are the most important things students can take away from their mathematics education (see Cuoco, Goldenberg & Mark, 1996; Cuoco, 1995; and Goldenberg, 1996 for more on this theme). For *all* students, whether they eventually build houses, run businesses, use spreadsheets, or prove theorems, the real utility of mathematics is not that you can use it to figure the slope of a wheelchair ramp, but that it provides you with the intellectual schemata necessary to make sense of a world in which the products of mathematical thinking are increasingly pervasive in almost every walk of life. This is not to say that other facets of mathematics should be neglected; questions of content, applications, cultural significance, and connections are all essential in the design of a mathematics program. But without explicit attention to mathematical ways of thinking, the goals of "intellectual sophistication" and "higher order thinking skills" will remain elusive.

The habits of mind approach seems to be gaining acceptance among other mathematics educators. *Everybody Counts* (NRC, 1989) describes it this way: "Mathematics offers distinctive modes of thought which are both versatile and powerful. . . . Experience with mathematical modes of thought builds mathematical power—a capacity of mind of increasing value in this technological age. . . ."

A curriculum that uses workplace and everyday tasks to support the goal of developing mathematical thinking is less likely to use the tasks *as* the curriculum; it is less likely to let the message "high school graduates should be able to solve problems like these" evolve into "high school graduates should be able to solve these problems." Conversely, a curriculum firmly rooted in concrete problems is less likely to turn the goal of developing mathematical habits of mind into a "mathematics appreciation" curriculum, that studies little more than lists of mathematical ways of thinking. The dialectic between problem-solving and theory-building is the fuel for progress in mathematics, and mathematics education should exploit its power. Problems can be both sources for and applications of methods, theories, and approaches that are characteristically mathematical. For example, through the work of Descartes, Euler, Lagrange, Galois, and many others, techniques for solving algebraic equations developed alongside theory about their solutions. (See, e.g., Kleiner, 1986.)

What does it mean to organize a curriculum around mathematical ways of thinking? One way to think about it is to imagine a common core curriculum for all students lasting through, say, grade 10. Students would work on problems, long-term investigations, and exercises very much as they do now, except the activities would be aimed at developing specific mathematical approaches.

In contrast to other kinds of organizers currently in use (applications, everyday situations, whimsy, even computational skill), the benchmark for deciding whether or not to include an activity in a curriculum would be the extent to which it provides an arena in which students can develop specific mathematical ways of thinking, such as:

- Algorithmic thinking: Constructing and using mechanical processes to model situations.

- Reasoning by continuity: Thinking about continuously varying systems.

- Combinatorial reasoning: Developing ways to "count without counting."

- Thought experiment: Learning to imagine complex interactions.

- Proportional reasoning: Thinking about scaling, area, measure, and probability.

- Reasoning about calculations: Developing algebraic thinking about properties of operations in various symbol systems.

- Topological thinking: Generalizing notions of closeness and approximation to non-metric situations.

These themes would run throughout the K-10 experience. They would be discussed explicitly in class, in diverse contexts, while students were working on problems. For example, an investigation involving topological reasoning might ask students to improve on the way users are allowed to organize their desktops in Macintosh and Windows environments.

After a decade of this core curriculum, students could choose from a set of electives that would vary from school to school and from year to year. Courses in probability, geometry, physics, history, algebra, cryptography, linear algebra, art, data-analysis, accounting, calculus, computer graphics, trigonometry, and whatever else interests teachers and students are all candidates. If students have a solid foundation in mathematical thinking, they will be prepared for a wide array of high-powered courses designed to meet the interests and needs of the entire spectrum of students. This is a genuine alternative to the current system of tracking: it would give students a choice and a chance to pursue their interests (16-year-old students *do* have well-developed interests). But no matter what choices they made, students would be assured of a substantial mathematics program that built on a core curriculum centering around mathematical habits of mind.

Such a curriculum would help students develop general strategies for doing mathematics, establish underlying mathematical (not just contextual) connections among the tasks, and help students develop the intellectual prowess necessary to deal with the kinds of problems they'll face after graduation. For example, a strand on algorithmic thinking would be a good context for investigating problems such as **Lottery Winnings** (p. 111) or **Buying on Credit** (p. 87). Whereas the contextual similarity of these tasks is evident even at a superficial level, they also share a deeper mathematical similarity based on a kind of algorithmic thinking that is somewhat removed from the mathematics backgrounds of most adults.

Show a group of eighth graders a table like Table 11-1. Then ask these eighth graders to describe what is going on. Their responses will be quite different from those of most adults who have been schooled in algebra. Adults immediately search for a "rule"—a procedure that can be performed to the "Input" column to produce the "Output" numbers. (In this case, multiplying by 5 and subtracting 1 does it). Young students are much more likely to see other patterns (the last digits on the right, for example), and very often they'll notice that every number in the right-hand column is 5 more than the one preceding it. This is the germ of *recursive thinking*, a very important way of looking at things. Rather than extinguish it during high school, a strand on algorithmic thinking would develop it in tandem with the more traditional "closed form" (multiply by 5 and subtract 1) way of modeling the data. Recursive approaches are ideal ways to build spreadsheets and model processes using computer algebra systems like *Mathematica*. And investigating the connections between recursive and closed form models can become a theme that organizes a great many of the topics in traditional high school mathematics.

Recursive thinking also gives students genuine intellectual power. Listen to a group of adults discussing the question, "How does the bank figure out the monthly payment on my car loan?" You'll hear qualitative statements, but you'll seldom hear a satisfactory mathematical description of what goes on behind the button on the calculator. Students accustomed to thinking in algorithms would ask themselves how the bank constructs a spreadsheet for computing the balance owed at the end of each month. They'd articulate an algorithm something like, "The amount you owe at the end of a month is the amount you owed at the beginning, plus 1/12 of the yearly interest on that amount, minus whatever you make for a payment." This simple model is easily executed on a spreadsheet, and it quickly leads to an algorithm for calculating the monthly payment on a loan. This can be refined in calculus to the method that is used in practice, and it can be modified well before calculus is known to handle tasks like those in this volume.

The usefulness of this kind of algorithmic thinking transcends the analysis of a particular context; algorithmic thinking is used by chefs, construction workers, librarians, and people surfing the Internet. A curriculum that focuses

TABLE 11-1: An input/output table	
INPUT	OUTPUT
1	4
2	9
3	14
4	19
5	24
6	29

on developing similar mathematical habits will go a long way toward achieving the goal of preparing students for challenges that don't yet exist. And it offers a mathematical framework that meets the goal of providing tasks that prepare students both for the world of work and for postsecondary education, that "exemplify central mathematical ideas," and that "convey the rich explanatory power of mathematics."

REFERENCES

Cuoco, A. (1995). Some worries about mathematics education. *Mathematics Teacher, 88*(3), 186-187.

Cuoco, A., Goldenberg, E. P., & Mark, J. (1996). Habits of mind: An organizing principle for mathematics curriculum. *The Journal of Mathematical Behavior, 15*(4), 375-403.

Goldenberg, E. P. (1996). "Habits of mind" as an organizer for the curriculum. *Boston University Journal of Education, 178*(1), 13-34.

Kleiner, I. (1986). The evolution of group theory: A brief survey. *Mathematics Magazine, 59*(4), 195-215.

National Research Council. (1989). *Everybody counts: A report to the nation on the future of mathematics education*. Washington, DC: National Academy Press.

ALBERT A. CUOCO is Senior Scientist and Director of the Mathematics Initiative at the Education Development Center (EDC). Before coming to EDC, he taught high school mathematics for 24 years to a wide range of students in the Woburn, Massachusetts, public schools, chairing the department for the last decade of his term. A student of Ralph Greenberg, Cuoco received his Ph.D. in mathematics from Brandeis in 1980. His mathematical interest and publications have been in algebraic number theory, although his recent work in high school geometry is gradually convincing him that geometric visualization has a place in mathematical thinking.

12 PREPARING STUDENTS FOR POSTSECONDARY EDUCATION

HARVEY B. KEYNES
UNIVERSITY OF MINNESOTA

The goals of *High School Mathematics at Work* are broad and ambitious as well as somewhat novel. This collection of essays discusses issues and potential themes for mathematical curricula that might be appropriate for both those students heading to the world of work and those headed into postsecondary education in the mathematical sciences. These issues and themes are illustrated by tasks that are intended to "exemplify central mathematical ideas" and "convey the rich explanatory power of mathematics."

One can hardly argue with any of these goals. But we also expect that the use of mathematics in the world of work by students who have completed their mathematics education in high school will probably be different (though not necessarily easier) than for students continuing in postsecondary education. In the first instance, technical workers might be expected to do concrete multi-step computations using numerical methods, probably with technological support, and to understand and use some algebraic and geometric methods, and symbolic arguments that are job-specific. They generally will not be expected to abstract and symbolically model mathematics embedded in work situations, to reason and communicate symbolically, or to use abstract mathematical reasoning or advanced mathematical tools in applications to other disciplines.

On the other hand, students moving on to postsecondary education, especially in careers that use mathematics in a professional capacity, will be expected to have these more conceptual skills as well as the some of the same concrete skills of students who enter the work force. Certainly in college courses, many of these more conceptual and abstract skills will be prerequisites. So a major issue for postsecondary preparation is whether tasks such as those in this volume can be used to effectively prepare students to engage in symbolic and abstract mathematical reasoning in algebra, geometry, and analysis as well as to explore concrete and numerical methods.

When selecting or designing tasks for inclusion in a curriculum, one must ask not only whether the tasks are based on rich and deep mathematics but also whether they can be used effectively in the typical classroom to exemplify central mathematical ideas and to contribute to an integrated whole. Can the rich and deep mathematical ideas embedded in tasks be exposed and effectively explored conceptually, visually, and analytically, as well as numerically and technologically, so that they contribute in meaningful ways to students' preparation for college calculus, combinatorics, and linear algebra? These questions depend on (a) the classroom teacher's interest and capability, (b) the mathematics curriculum, (c) classroom dynamics, (d) school and family expectations, and (e) the inherent mathematical ideas embedded in the tasks themselves. Any task must be viewed in this larger perspective to see if it can really be useful in helping students learn mathematics at both the concrete/computational and symbolic/conceptual levels.

It does not take very long to realize the difficulty of finding tasks that can effectively illustrate the major objectives of this document. Such tasks must, at a minimum,

- be presented in a practical context in language that is easily understood but precise;

- be amenable to analysis on several different levels: numerically, geometrically, symbolically, and conceptually;

- be based at least partially on mathematics that is of central importance in the high school curriculum; and

- allow for more extended mathematical interpretations.

The first point, which concerns linguistic style and clarity of mathematical goals, needs some amplification. Poorly worded and mathematically vague tasks actually discourage students from seeking to develop and analyze the mathematical models behind these questions and encourage them simply to resort to ad hoc or strictly computational solutions. If high school students were really able to interpret mathematically these verbal descriptions, many of the widespread student difficulties with "story" problems would suddenly vanish.

One needs to remember that the abstraction of the mathematical phenomena described by seemingly straightforward language is one of the most difficult tasks of applied mathematics, even for professional mathematicians.

In examining a task, our primary concern is to determine what mathematics students can learn from it. Many of the tasks in this document have the capacity to be mathematically analyzed both concretely and conceptually at levels that support both work force and post-secondary goals. **Lottery Winnings** (p. 111) is an excellent illustration: one can feel reasonably confident that many teachers will encourage students both to explore numerical solutions and also to conceptualize the important mathematical ideas embedded in this task.

Given a collection of tasks, one important measure is the breadth of mathematics present in the tasks. Clearly, any small collection of tasks will necessarily need to make choices and de-emphasize certain aspects. As a whole, the tasks in this volume use classical geometric patterns and some level of pictorial representations. Algebraic reasoning at a classical level is also addressed. On the other hand, newer uses of geometric and visual reasoning—information embedded in pictures or graphs—are downplayed. Moreover, the breadth required for vocational training or direct entry into the work world is certainly different for students who will become professional users of mathematics. These tasks can provide a piece of the picture but not the entire spectrum of mathematical expectation for all postsecondary students.

Many of the tasks in this document meet conditions listed above. Here are three more tasks:

- You are installing track lighting in an old warehouse that is being remodeled into a restaurant. The lights can adequately illuminate up to 15 feet from the bulbs and, at that distance, illuminate a circle with a 6 foot diameter. Figure out where to place the tracks and the bulbs for maximum illumination of the customer area. This task uses geometry, trigonometry, solid geometry (looking at the cone of illumination from a constrained light bulb), and proportional reasoning. It could be modeled with computer software or solved analytically. All of the mathematics involved is within the scope of the high school curriculum.

- Your employer at your first job has given you a choice of where to invest your retirement funds: in a mutual fund that is expected to grow at 10% per year or at the local bank, which charges a 1% yearly service rate for a similar fund, also rated at 10%. You would like to deal with your local bank but don't want to lose too much money. Suppose you expect to put $1,000 each year into the fund. How much will you lose over 10 or 20 or 30 years if you invest at your local bank? This task, which can be modeled in many different ways, illustrates the famous rule that a 1% difference in interest grows very rapidly in compounding over time. It can also lead to some interesting graphs and comparisons of growth rates of functions. Finally, it can be explained in language appropriate for a high school classroom.

- Analyze a contour map with peaks and flat areas. This will provide an opportunity to study curves and shapes in two-dimensions, explore rates of change (closely packed contours), preview functions and graphs on the plane, and examine the geometry of three-space. Practical aspects from cartography and local area maps can provide an everyday context.

The overall goal of *High School Mathematics at Work*—to call attention to rich and compelling manifestations of high school mathematics all around us—is enticing and potentially very important. And, in addressing a broad and diverse set of students, it is reasonable to downplay the role of abstraction. Yet many mathematicians and mathematics educators would argue that mathematics without abstraction is not mathematics. While this dictum could be argued as applying to all students, it is probably less controversial to apply it to postsecondary students who will be professional users of mathematics.

The process of developing tasks with "real life" contexts that are relevant and mathematically significant both for students directly entering the technical work force and for students going on to mathematics-based careers is both difficult and daunting. We must continue to discuss issues and directions, such as scope, breadth, language, and complexity of the mathematics. The tasks in this volume do, however, provide an excellent core framework and standard of quality in which to continue the discussion.

HARVEY B. KEYNES received his B.A. in 1962 from the University of Pennsylvania and the Ph.D. in 1966 from Wesleyan University. His research interests are in dynamical systems. He has directed the following projects: University of Minnesota Talented Youth Mathematics Program (UMTYMP, state and private funding); the National Science Foundation's (NSF) Teacher Renewal Project; the NSF-supported Minnesota Mathematics Mobilization; the Ford Foundation Urban Mathematics Collaborative; the NSF-supported Mathematics in Education Reform Network; the NSF-supported Young Scholars Project; the Bush Foundation to increase female participation in UMTYMP; and the NSF-funded Early Alert Initiative. He is the recipient of the 1992 Award for Distinguished Public Service of the American Mathematical Society. He is published extensively in mathematics education journals.

TASK. A lottery winner died after five of the twenty years in which he was to receive annual payments on a $5 million winning. At the time of his death, he had just received the fifth payment of $250,000. Because the man did not have a will, the judge ordered the remaining lottery proceeds to be auctioned and set the minimum bid at $1.3 million. Why was the minimum bid set so low? How much would you be willing to bid for the lottery proceeds?

COMMENTARY. This task engages students in exploration of interest rates, exponential growth, and formulating financial questions in mathematical terms. These ideas introduce students to an important way of thinking about decisions they will have to make throughout their lives. For example, students will need to decide whether they can afford to buy a car and, if so, whether it would be better to lease; or whether to go to college now versus working first. Later in life, sound decisions can come from an understanding of annuities and, more generally, the present value of future money. Many will live in homes for which funds need to be saved for future repairs; others will need to consider the pros and cons of renting versus buying. Students should learn to consider all aspects of such decisions, including cost of loans, loss of earning power, and effects of inflation.

These issues bear directly on civic life as well. Every community thinks about bond issues that provide money for capital improvements. This involves, among other things, depreciation of capital expenditures. How do you think about borrowing vs. paying up front? Consideration and discussion of these issues can make students better citizens and more informed voters.

The mathematical formulation of the problem depends on recursive thinking, an important tool in many applications of mathematics. This task is especially appropriate because it can be explored at many levels of mathematical sophistication. The solution presented below, however, assumes only enough algebra to be able to enter formulas in a spreadsheet.

MATHEMATICAL ANALYSIS. One way to think about this problem is to imagine an equivalent scenario. Suppose you make an initial deposit in a bank account at a fixed rate of interest and then withdraw $250,000 each year for 15 years. This is equivalent because buying the lottery proceeds will produce the same stream of payments. The question, then, is how much must be deposited at the beginning so that there will be enough to last exactly 15 more years.

There are 15 remaining payments of $250,000 each, totaling $3,750,000. But a deposit of $3.75 million would be more than is necessary because it would collect a substantial amount of interest, especially in the beginning years. In order to make some specific calculations, one can assume a fixed interest rate of 8% and then ask whether the judge's suggested $1.3 million will be enough. Since the year five payment has just been made, one can reasonably assume that the year six payment will occur exactly one year later. At year six, then, the initial deposit will have accrued 8% interest, which amounts to $.08 \times \$1,300,000 = \$104,000$. At the same time that interest payment is made, however, one would be withdrawing the year six payment of $250,000. That leaves $1,300,000 + \$104,000 - \$250,000 = \$1,154,000$ remaining in the account at year six. A spreadsheet can be used to continue these calculations for subsequent years. If the initial payment is in cell C5, the formula for cell C6 is C5+C5*.08–250000. That formula may then be copied to cells C7 and below.

TABLE 1: Remaining principal by year, first attempt		
YEAR	PAYMENT	PRINCIPAL REMAINING
5		$1,300,000.00
6	$250,000	$1,154,000.00
7	$250,000	$996,320.00
8	$250,000	$826,025.60
9	$250,000	$642,107.65
10	$250,000	$443,476.26
11	$250,000	$228,954.36
12	$250,000	–$2,729.29

Table 1 shows that if the initial deposit is $1.3 million, and the interest rate is 8%, there will not be enough to make the payment in year 12, never mind years 13 through 20. Note that although 1.3 million could provide only a little more than 5 payments of $250,000 if there were no interest, it can provide almost 8 payments at an interest rate of 8%. Thus, The judge's initial bid is lower than $3.75 million in order to account for the interest that will accrue. If an interest rate of 8% is reasonable, however, $1.3 million is far too low.

What we want to find is an initial deposit that will leave exactly $0 at the end of the year 20. We know that $3.75 million is too high, and $1.3 million is too low. By choos-

ing initial deposit amounts between these, and keeping track of which are too low and which are too high, we can "zero in" on the desired value. According to Table 2, $2,139,869.67 almost works. In fact, to the closest penny, it is the best answer.

Thus, assuming a fixed 8% interest rate, this stream of payments is worth $2,139,869.67 today. Another way to say this is that assuming an 8% discount rate, the *present value* of the payments is $2,139,869.67.

One of the nice features of this task is that there are many answers, depending upon the interest rate chosen, and many approaches to solutions, depending upon the students' knowledge. The discussion above, for example, can be phrased in more sophisticated mathematical notation. The spreadsheet formula might be written $D_{n+1} = (1+i) D_n - P$, where i is the annual interest rate, P is the $250,000 annual payment the lottery winner was receiving and D_n is the amount of money still invested at year n in order to produce the annual payments. Then the goal would be to find what initial investment in year five, D_5, just covers the 15 years of payments, leading to D_{20} being $0.

Students who are prone to exploring the capabilities of their spreadsheet software might find a "Present Value" function which gives the desired initial investment directly. Other students, after studying geometric series, might derive or use the present value formula,

$$D = \frac{(1 + i)^N - 1}{i(1 + i)^N} P$$

where N is the number of payments, and the other variables are as above. Many

TABLE 2: Remaining principal by year, final attempt		
YEAR	PAYMENT	PRINCIPAL REMAINING
5		$2,139,869.67
6	$250,000	$2,061,059.24
7	$250,000	$1,975,943.98
8	$250,000	$1,884,019.50
9	$250,000	$1,784,741.06
10	$250,000	$1,677,520.35
11	$250,000	$1,561,721.97
12	$250,000	$1,436,659.73
13	$250,000	$1,301,592.51
14	$250,000	$1,155,719.91
15	$250,000	$998,177.50
16	$250,000	$828,031.71
17	$250,000	$644,274.24
18	$250,000	$445,816.18
19	$250,000	$231,481.48
20	$250,000	–$0.01

mathematics of finance texts contain derivations of this formula. This task could be used to motivate such formulas and functions.

EXTENSIONS. Explore what the necessary initial payment would be when different interest rates are assumed. Does the initial payment go up or down as the interest rate goes up? Why does the answer make sense? Find the interest rate, if possible, for which the judge's suggested bid of $1.3 million makes sense.

Assuming that students use a "search" procedure for finding the initial payment, ask about the efficiency of different methods of searching. Some students, for example, might try $1.4 million, $1.5 million, $1.6 million, and $1.7 million—clearly an inefficient approach when $1.3 million was already known to be far too low. Explore the mathematics behind the binary search method, in which the next guess is always the average of the best high and low guesses so far. Explore the mathematics behind the linear interpolation search method, in which the next guess is determined by finding the intercept of the line between the best high and low guesses so far.

If students are impatient with a "search" procedure, ask them to use algebra to find a formula. The algebra involved in the derivation of the formula requires use of some standard facts about geometric series, and might provide motivation for the usefulness of such formulas.

Suppose a student inherits money or wins a lottery. This money provides a certain annual income for a fixed number of years. How much of the income should be put aside so that the winner will still have savings long after the annual payments cease? Can it last a lifetime? Can it last indefinitely? It is also interesting to consider the impact of taxes and inflation. (These are serious problems. A research study of the early winners of lotteries showed that more than 75% were broke 20 years after winning.)

LOTTERY WINNINGS (CONTINUED)

This task and its extensions can provide opportunities for exploration and discussion of other financial instruments, such as annuities, pensions, mortgages, and other savings and borrowing plans, and also economic issues, such as interest rates, other rates of return, the trade-off between risk and expected return, and the liquidity of an investment. Rather than leading to a unit on finance, questions about these issues can lead students to be interested in the mathematics behind them.

HOSPITAL QUALITY

TASK. As health care director for your company, your job is to select which of two local hospitals you will send your employees to in case of emergency. Mercy Hospital is the larger of the two and a local emergency care facility. It had 2,100 surgery patients last year, many of whom entered the hospital in poor condition. Of its surgery patients, 63 died. Excelsior is smaller. It had 800 surgery patients last year, a smaller percentage entered in poor condition, and 16 of its surgery patients died. The detailed information is given in Table 1.

COMMENTARY. This is a decision-making situation that might actually arise in the workplace, but its relevance is much broader. Drawing sound conclusions in such situations requires understanding and careful thinking. In the news and in everyday life, we are inundated with statistics supporting various positions. Thus, it is important that students learn to look for complexities that are often hidden behind the statistics.

Both directors of public relations are correct, despite their seemingly contradictory state-

TABLE 1: Patient mortality, two hospitals				
	MERCY HOSPITAL		**EXCELSIOR HOSPITAL**	
	PATIENTS	**DEATHS**	**PATIENTS**	**DEATHS**
In Good Condition	600	6	600	8
In Poor Condition	1,500	57	200	8
Combined Total	2,100	63	800	16

The director of public relations at Excelsior claims that the overall death rate at Excelsior is smaller than the overall death rate at Mercy and that the intimacy of a small hospital is preferable to the hustle and bustle of a large facility. The director of public relations at Mercy claims that if you look at the death rates more carefully, you will see that they are a better facility—they simply treat a lot of patients who are more seriously ill.

Analyze the given data and make a recommendation to your board of directors. Make the recommendation in the form of a memo in which you clearly justify your decision, knowing that the director of the hospital you do not choose may appeal your decision.

ments. These data provide an example of an occurrence known in probability as Simpson's paradox; it can also occur in other situations involving "weighted averages." Similar apparent paradoxes arise, for example, in situations where women or minorities in various jobs earn about the same as their male counterparts, but their overall average earnings may be far less. (This can happen if most women are employed in low paying jobs, for example.)

Because of the apparent paradox, this task provides an intriguing context for discussing more fundamental notions, such as probability, rates, and weighted averages. Working through such examples can sensitize students to the need to understand the numbers and trends that give rise to statistics. It will also give them a better sense of what to believe and what to question when confronted with statistical assertions.

MATHEMATICAL ANALYSIS. To check the directors' assertions, one must compute death rates. For example, the death rate for patients in good condition at Mercy is 6/600 or 1%. The other results are shown in Table 2.

recruit women for the low-paying positions, and hard to recruit them for the high-paying positions, it is possible that the average salary for women will still be lower than the average salary for men, seemingly contradicting the company's intent to pay women more.

EXTENSIONS. Students might find and analyze employment and salary patterns in various professions. They might look at admissions rates at a university by gender or

TABLE 2: Patient mortality, two hospitals, with rates						
	MERCY HOSPITAL			EXCELSIOR HOSPITAL		
	PATIENTS	DEATHS	RATE	PATIENTS	DEATHS	RATE
In Good Condition	600	6	1%	600	8	1.33%
In Poor Condition	1500	57	3.8%	200	8	4%
Combined Total	2100	63	3%	800	16	2%

Looking only at the combined death rate, it looks like Excelsior is the better hospital, for a 2% death rate is better than 3%. Looking at the separate death rates, however, the picture is different. For patients in good condition, the death rate is lower at Mercy. Similarly, a patient in poor condition is better off at Mercy. So the public relations director at Mercy is correct: Mercy Hospital has a better success rate both with patients in good health and with those in poor health. The reason Mercy loses more patients overall is that it treats many more seriously ill patients.

Here's an easy way to see how averages based on aggregates can deliver a different message than averages based on components. Suppose a company, in an attempt to recruit women into all positions, pays them more than men in all positions. If it is easy to

by race, for the university as a whole, and then separated by college or by department. Such assignments should not be given, however, without allowing for discussion of equity issues that can be raised by such data.

Students might construct data that illustrates analogous paradoxes in contexts that appeal to them. In baseball, for example, it is possible for a batter to have the best batting average before the all-star break and the best average after the all-star break and yet fail to have the best average for the whole season.

Students might also explore other instances of weighted averages, perhaps first as simple ways of computing more familiar averages. For example, if a teacher explains that homework counts 50%, each of three exams count 10%, and the final exam counts 20%, a student can determine his or her average going into the final as follows:

$$\frac{50 \cdot Homework + 10 \cdot Exam_1 + 10 \cdot Exam_2 + 10 \cdot Exam_3}{50 + 10 + 10 + 10}$$

The arithmetic in this task deserves comment. If one thinks of the death rates as fractions, then one might consider the relationship between the separate death rates and the combined death rate to be like addition. In the case of Mercy hospital, the "addition" looks as follows, where the ⊕ indicates that this is not the standard addition of fractions.

$$\frac{6}{600} \oplus \frac{57}{1500} = \frac{63}{2100}$$

Notice that this "addition" is performed by adding the numerators and adding denominators—one of the mistakes that students make when they are supposed to perform the standard addition of fractions. Yet, this "addition" is used in many contexts, from computing batting averages in baseball to computing terms in Farey sequences, an advanced topic in number theory.

Students might be asked, "Why does this 'addition' make sense here?" "What is the difference between this and the standard addition of fractions?" "What is different about the contexts that gives rise to a different kind of addition?" Discussion of such questions can provide for a firmer understanding of the concepts of fraction, rate, and average.

This kind of "addition by component" is reminiscent of addition of vectors, which gives us a geometric model of the situation. The data for patients in good condition at Mercy (600 patients, 6 deaths) can be represented as the vector (600, 6) which can be represented geometrically as an arrow from the origin to the point (600, 6) on a coordinate plane. (See Figure 1.) Then the death rate, 6/600, is precisely the slope of the vector. By similarly representing the data for patients in poor condition as the vector (1500, 57), the sum of the vectors is given by adding the components of the vectors. That is, (600, 6) + (1500, 57) = (2100, 63). Geometrically, the sum of these vectors is the diagonal of the parallelogram formed by the vectors. (See Figure 1.) Note that because the death rate is represented by the slope of the vector, a steeper vector corresponds to a higher death rate. We can similarly represent the data from Excelsior Hospital (Figure 2).

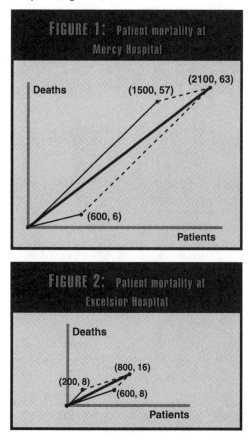

FIGURE 1: Patient mortality at Mercy Hospital

FIGURE 2: Patient mortality at Excelsior Hospital

Superimposing the data from Excelsior Hospital upon that from Mercy (Figure 3) shows that the sides of the Excelsior parallelogram are steeper than the corresponding sides of the Mercy parallelogram, but Mercy has a steeper diagonal. To gain a spatial and kinesthetic sense of this paradox, students might use dynamic geometry software to draw such a picture to construct data that exhibit this paradox.

Observe that the diagonal representing the sum must be between the two vectors, indicating that the slope of the sum must be between the other slopes. This provides a compelling geometric argument for the algebraic fact that $\frac{a}{b} \oplus \frac{c}{d}$, defined as above, is always between the two fractions a/b and

c/d, as long as a, b, c, and d are all positive. Proving this algebraically, on the other hand, requires some non-obvious techniques.

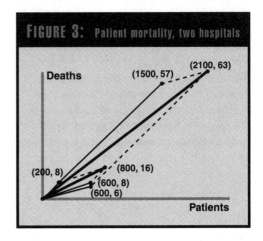

FIGURE 3: Patient mortality, two hospitals

Rounding Off

TASK. In a certain multi-million dollar company, Division Managers are required to submit monthly detail and summary expense reports on which the amounts are rounded, for ease of reading, to the closest $1,000. One month, a Division Manager's detail report shows $1,000 for printing and $1,000 for copying. In the summary report, the total for "printing and copying" is listed as $3,000. When questioned about it by the Vice President, he claims that the discrepancy is merely round-off error. In subsequent months, the Vice President notices that such round-off errors seem to happen often on this Division Manager's reports. Before the Vice President asks that the Division Manager re-create the reports without rounding, she wants to know how often this should happen.

COMMENTARY. We are often quoted rounded numbers that do not then turn out to be quite exact. Even a bank's approximate computational program for principal and interest can eventually drift far enough off the actual payment for the difference to be important. In any problem, we have to be concerned about which numbers are exact and about the accuracy of those that are not.

People don't often realize how huge the consequences of rounding numbers can be. Suppose, for example, that a company's board of directors has received a report indicating that each of the machines manufactured by their company will take up 2% of the freight capacity of their cargo planes, and the board wants to know how many machines can be shipped on each plane. In our standard notation, 2% represents a number somewhere between 1.5% and 2.5%. Solving the problem with each of these two exact percentages yields answers that are

quite different. Using 1.5%, the board will find that the plane can hold 100% ÷ (1.5%/machine) ≈ 66 machines; but by using 2.5%, the board will find that the plane can hold 100% ÷ (2.5%/machine) = 40 machines. So, in truth, all the board can say is that the answer is between 40 and 66 machines! Clearly, the report has not supplied accurate enough information, especially if the profitability of the shipment depends strongly on the number of machines that can be shipped.

If, on the other hand, the report had indicated that the board could assume another decimal place of accuracy, by stating that each machine accounted for 2.0% of the plane's capacity, then, with rounding, the board can be sure that the exact portion is somewhere between 1.95% and 2.05%. Using these exact percentages, the board can conclude that the plane can hold between 48 and 51 machines. One decimal place of additional accuracy in the reported data reduced the uncertainty in the answer from 26 machines to 3.

This problem is important for another reason as well, for its solution introduces a useful mathematical connection: the notion of geometric probability, where the range of options (technically, the "sample space") is represented by a geometric figure so that the probability of certain events correspond to the areas of certain portions of that figure. Geometric probability enables us to use our knowledge of the area (or length or volume) of geometric figures to compute probabilities.

MATHEMATICAL ANALYSIS. Fundamental to an understanding of geometric probability is the idea that on a portion of a line, probability is proportional to length, and on a region in a plane, probability is proportional to area. For example, suppose that in Figure 1, the areas of regions A, B, and C are 2, 1, and 3 respectively, for a total area of 6. Then a point picked at random from these regions would have probability of 2/6, 1/6, and 3/6 of being in regions A, B, and C respectively.

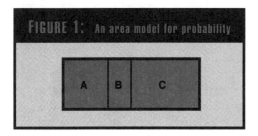

FIGURE 1: An area model for probability

Note that the boundaries of the regions are not significant in the calculations because they have no area. Ideally (as opposed to in a physical model) these boundaries are lines with no thickness. Thus, the probability that a point from this rectangle will lie *exactly* on one of these boundaries, rather than close to a boundary, is zero.

In order to answer the question at hand, it must be stated more mathematically: Given a pair of numbers that both round to 1, and assuming that all such pairs are equally likely, find the probability that their sum rounds to 2. This assumption may or may not be reasonable in a particular business and would require some knowledge of typical expenses and some non-mathematical judgment.

A number that rounds to 1 is somewhere between .5 and 1.5. These numbers may be represented by a line segment, shown as the shaded portion of the number line in Figure 2.

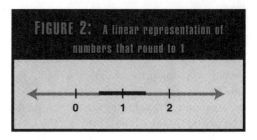

FIGURE 2: A linear representation of numbers that round to 1

To state this a bit more formally, a number x will be rounded to 1 if $.5 < x < 1.5$. (Again, we can ignore the boundaries, .5 and 1.5, because the probability that a number will be exactly on the boundary is zero.) Suppose y also rounds to 1, so that $.5 < y < 1.5$. If we consider a coordinate plane with points (x, y), these two inequalities determine a square of side 1. This square (Figure 3) represents all pairs of numbers where both could be rounded to 1. For example, point A represents $(.8, .6)$, B represents $(1.1, 1.1)$, and C represents $(1.3, 1.4)$.

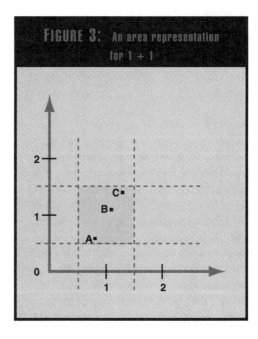

FIGURE 3: An area representation for 1 + 1

What can we say about $x + y$ for points inside the square? Most of the time, $x + y$ will round to 2, but sometimes it will round to 3, and sometimes it will round to 1. Note that the components of A add to 1.4, which rounds to 1; the components of B add to 2.3, which rounds to 2; and the components of C add to 2.7, which rounds to 3.

The probability that $1 + 1$ rounds to 1 is the fraction of the square containing pairs that, when added, round to 1. Now, $x + y$ rounds to 1 if $x + y < 1.5$, which will occur for points below the line $x + y = 1.5$. Similarly, $x + y$ rounds to 3 for points above the line $x + y = 2.5$. These conditions each cut off a triangular corner of the square (shown as the darker shaded regions in Figure 4).

The legs of these right triangles are each of length 1/2, so they each have area 1/8. Thus,

the probability that $1 + 1 = 3$ is 1/8, and the probability that $1 + 1 = 1$ is also 1/8. Finally the probability that $1 + 1 = 2$ is 3/4, the remaining fraction of the square.

EXTENSIONS. What's the probability that $1 \times 1 = 2$? This requires calculating the portion of the square that satisfies $xy > 1.5$ (Figure 5). Is this bigger or smaller than 1/8, calculated as the area of the upper triangle in Figure 4? A comparison of Figures 4 and 5 shows remarkable similarity. What is the precise relationship between the line $x + y = 2.5$ and the curve $xy = 1.5$? Solving the first equation for y and substituting into the second yields $x(x - 2.5) = 1.5$, a quadratic which simplifies to $-x^2 + 2.5x - 1.5 = 0$ or $2x^2 - 5x + 3 = 0$. This second equation factors easily as $(2x - 3)(x - 1) = 0$, yielding solutions $x = 1.5$ and $x = 1$. These solutions imply that the line $x + y = 2.5$ and the curve $xy = 1.5$ intersect the square at the same points. By the concavity

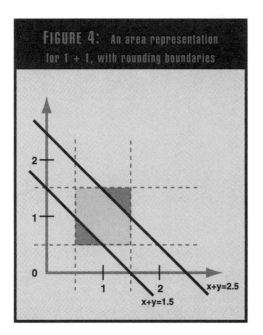

FIGURE 4: An area representation for 1 + 1, with rounding boundaries

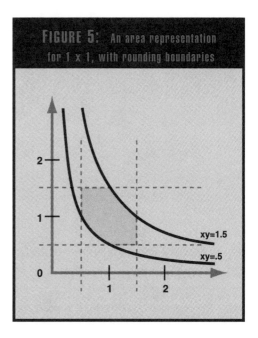

FIGURE 5: An area representation for 1 x 1, with rounding boundaries

of the curve $xy = 1.5$, the curve must lie below the line inside the square. So the answer should be a little bigger than $1/8 = .125$.

Calculus allows us to calculate the shaded area as precisely:

$$\int_{1}^{1.5} (1.5 - 1.5/x) \, dx = .75 - 1.5 \ln 1.5 \approx .142.$$

Similarly, if $x = .6$ and $y = .7$, then $xy = .42 < .5$, which would round to 0. The probability that xy rounds to 0 is $.5 \ln 2 - .25 \approx .097$.

What about 1/1? It rounds to 0 with probability .0625, to 1 with probability .75, to 2 with probability .175, and to 3 with probability .0125. These calculations require only geometry, no calculus.

RULES OF THUMB

TASK. Some drivers learn the rule of thumb, "Follow two car lengths behind for every 10 miles per hour." Others learn, "Stay two seconds behind the car ahead." Do these two rules give the same results? Is one safer than the other? Is one better for roads with speed limits of 45 or 50 miles per hour and another for highways on which the speed limit is 65 or 70 miles per hour?

COMMENTARY. Obtaining a driver's license has become one of the "rites of passage" in the U.S. On almost every written driver's test, applicants are asked how closely one driver should follow another on the highway. We all appreciate the dangers of tailgating—not enough stopping time and not enough space to avoid an accident. However, it is not clear that there is agreement about what actually constitutes tailgating— how far apart cars should be.

Rules of thumb are helpful guidelines— sometimes derived from experience—that are calculated using easily available measurements. Often they are developed under particular conditions and may be extremely inaccurate if those conditions are not fulfilled. The existence of two rules of thumb for the same situation suggests a natural question: Are the two rules simply two different ways of saying the same thing or are they offering different advice? As stated, the rules may provide visual images of how far to stay behind another car, but translating that understanding into practice on the road may be quite a different matter. The exercise of interpreting rules of thumb and comparing their results with real data could help students realize that the rules they use have implications for their actions. Also, there is the reality of high incidences of automobile accidents among new drivers. This exercise

may help students examine and improve their driving habits.

In order to do the task, students need to know what it means to make a comparison. They have to identify the quantities needed in order to calculate the following distances given by the two rules and represent the rules mathematically. There are many ways to do this—written descriptions, tables, equations, or graphs, all basic tools of mathematical literacy. A comparison requires that the two representations use the same units of measurement—hence some conversions are necessary from the units used in the original rules of thumb. Such conversions are an essential part of many everyday situations, both at work and at home.

MATHEMATICAL ANALYSIS. To begin, students might be well advised to consider the case in which two automobiles are traveling at a steady rate. The information presented is not complete and students will find that they have to seek out missing data. Naturally, what students seek will depend on their interpretation of the task. One necessary piece of information may be average car length.

The units for the car-length rule are miles per hour and car lengths, and the units for the two-second rule are miles per hour and seconds. To compare the two rules, both need to be written in the same units. A typical sedan is about 14 feet, so the car-length rule might be translated as "follow about 28 feet behind for every 10 miles per hour" or as the equation $y = 28(x/10)$, where x is the speed of the car in miles per hour and y is the following distance in feet.

If a car is traveling at x mph, then it travels x miles in one hour—in other words, $x/3600$

miles in one second. The two-second rule is then "if your speed is x mph, follow about $2x/3600$ miles behind." As an equation, it is $z = 2(x/3600)$, where x is again the speed of the car in miles per hour, but this time z is the following distance in miles (not feet as in the previous equation), and we use a different letter to distinguish it from y above.

Now the rules are both in terms of miles per hour and units of distance but not the same units of distance. The car-length rule is as follows:

$$y = 28(x/10),$$

where y is the following distance in feet. The two-second rule is

$$z = 2(x/3600),$$

where z is the following distance in miles. Simplifying the car-length rule gives

$$y = 2.8x,$$

where y is the following distance in feet. Simplifying the two-second rule gives

$$z = x/1800,$$

where z is the following distance in miles.

Now it's a matter of converting z to feet (or y to miles). There are 5,280 feet in a mile, so $x/1800$ miles is $5280(x/1800)$ feet. That's about $2.93x$ feet—very close to the distance given by the car-length rule!

Some driver's manuals give data on the distance cars travel before they are able to come to a complete stop. Often the distance is broken into two components, the reaction

distance and the braking distance. The reaction distance is the distance traveled while the driver reacts to a situation and hits the brakes. The braking distance is the distance traveled from the time the brakes are applied until the car comes to a stop. A simplified version is given in Table 1.

TABLE 1: Reaction and braking distances for various speeds		
SPEED	REACTION DISTANCE	BRAKING DISTANCE
20 mph	20 feet	20 feet
30 mph	30 feet	45 feet
40 mph	40 feet	80 feet
50 mph	50 feet	125 feet
60 mph	60 feet	180 feet

This table allows a comparison of the distances given by the rules of thumb with actual stopping distances. But the stopping distances are the distances required for a car to stop before hitting an immovable object blocking the road, whereas the rules of thumb assume that the car in front is also moving forward. This table suggests some questions about the rules of thumb: How much reaction time does each rule allow? Why are the rules of thumb linear and the stopping distances non-linear—and does this matter?

EXTENSIONS. In 1977, a *National Observer* article stated, "The usual rule of thumb in the real-estate business is that a family can afford a house 2 to $2\frac{1}{2}$ times its income." Incomes and housing prices have changed considerably since 1977, and real-estate agents' rules of thumb may have changed as well. Every subject—from shop to physics, from auto mechanics to economics—introduces rules of thumb that work well in appropriate situations. Even in mathematics, practices that students don't understand may acquire the status of rules of thumb for them and may be misapplied.

The original rule of thumb gave the measurement of a person's waist in terms of the measurements of their thumb, wrist, or neck. "Twice around the thumb is once around the wrist. Twice around the wrist is once around the neck. Twice around the neck is once around the waist." (The Dutch refer to "rules of fist," possibly for similar reasons.) The differences in body proportions at different ages (see Figure 1) suggest that this rule may have been developed for adults and may not be useful in designing clothes for young children. Students can be asked to create a rule that would work for young children. Because children's proportions change so rapidly with age, such a rule might include age as a variable.

There are numerous other rules of thumb: "The rule of 72" in finance, "Double the tax to get the tip" in a restaurant, "Magnetic north is true north" in navigation, and so on. Students can compare the results of these rules with actual data or investigate the accuracy and derivation of such rules in their areas of interest. For instance, *The Joy of Cooking* provides the following rule of thumb for cooking turkeys, "allow 20 to 25 minutes per pound for birds up to 6 pounds. For larger birds, allow 15 to 20 minutes per pound. For birds weighing over 16 pounds, allow 13 to 15 minutes per pound. In any case, add about 5 minutes to the pound if the bird you are cooking is stuffed" (Rombauer & Becker, 1976). Students could explore the reasonableness of such predictions: might one conclude that a 5.9 pound bird requires (5.9) × (25) = 147.5 minutes, while a 6.1 pound bird requires no more than (6.1) × (20) = 122 minutes?

There are many other natural variations on the original problem as well. How sensitive is the car-length rule to what is assumed about the length of a car? Is the difference in average length of European versus U.S. sedans important to this rule of thumb? How should the two rules be modified for use on wet pavement? Questions might be raised about what happens if one car is traveling faster than the other or about the relationship between age and reaction time. In a state with a large number of retirees such as Florida, should the rules of thumb be the same as those in states with younger populations?

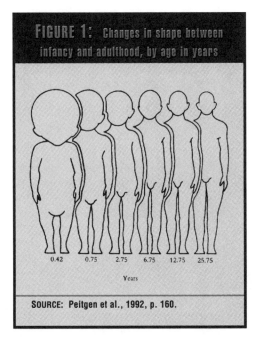

FIGURE 1: Changes in shape between infancy and adulthood, by age in years

0.42 0.75 2.75 6.75 12.75 25.75

Years

SOURCE: Peitgen et al., 1992, p. 160.

RULES OF THUMB (CONTINUED)

Another issue concerns the usability of the two rules for following distance. If the two rules give essentially the same advice, is one easier to use in practice than the other? Is it easier to think in terms of distance measured in car lengths, picturing the space filled with cars, or to pick a marker such as a road sign or billboard, and count seconds? Opinions will vary as to which is the easier method.

REFERENCES

Peitgen, H.-O. et al. (1992). *Fractals for the classroom*. New York: Springer-Verlag.

Rombauer, I. S. & Becker, M. R. (1976). *The joy of cooking*. New York: Bobbs-Merrill Company.

PART FOUR

IMPLICATIONS FOR TEACHING AND TEACHER EDUCATION

OVERVIEW

For many experienced and prospective teachers, tasks like those in *High School Mathematics at Work* pose several inter-related challenges involving curriculum, pedagogy, and assessment.

- In planning the class: How can I tell if a task is appropriate for my students? How would such tasks fit in my curriculum? After choosing a task, what are the mathematical concepts and big ideas that can be approached with the task?

- During class: How do I get students working on the task I've chosen? What can I expect from classroom discussion? How can I engage all students in the big mathematical ideas?

- After class: What *can* I expect from student work? What *should* I expect from student work? How should I provide feedback?

These questions speak to the broad demands that today's students and curricula place on teachers. To respond adequately to these demands, teachers must be very resourceful and must have the skills and inclinations to create an intellectual community in their classrooms. What is needed is teachers who are mathematically confident and have the tools to learn mathematics as they need it, so that they and their students may thrive when either the curriculum or the students take them into uncharted territory. Furthermore, teachers need professional support in creating learning communities of teachers in their schools, districts, and states.

Working with both preservice and inservice teachers, the authors of the essays in Part Four find that tasks like those in this document have changed teachers' ideas about students' capabilities, about how a curriculum might be organized, and about what it means to do mathematics. In each case, such change requires time and support.

The *Professional Standards for Teaching Mathematics* (National Council of Teachers of Mathematics, 1991) acknowledges the important role that teachers have in choosing tasks in their curriculum. Under the heading "Worthwhile Mathematical Tasks," it asserts that

The teacher of mathematics should pose tasks that are based on—

- sound and significant mathematics;

- knowledge of students' understandings, interests, and experiences;

- knowledge of the range of ways that diverse students learn mathematics. (p. 25)

In her essay, Glenda Lappan suggests that "teachers are architects of curriculum," for what is learned depends upon the context in which it is taught. She acknowledges that the use of complex problems creates more complexity in classrooms, and she notes that if preservice teachers work through complex problems themselves, they receive some of the background and confidence they need to handle such complexity. After describing problem-centered teaching and some of the issues that it raises, Lappan suggests that "teachers will find that learning alone is unlikely to be as powerful as engaging in dialogue with other teachers."

Like Lappan, Gilbert Cuevas acknowledges that with scant experience solving complex mathematical tasks, many preservice teachers are uncertain about using such tasks in their classrooms. He presents five principles for the preparation of teachers, such as providing "opportunity for reflection about their tasks and their implementation with students," and emphasizing communication, discussion, and orientation toward problems.

Paul LeMahieu and Marshá Horton note that assessments alone are not effective agents of educational reform. When extended, open-ended tasks are included in assessment, however, there is an opportunity for a different and powerful role, if teachers are involved in the evaluation of student work responding to these items. LeMahieu and Horton discuss how teachers develop consensus about quality and rigorous expectations for quality through discussions of student work on assessments. Furthermore, they note, inservice teachers' expectations for students change when they participate in such scoring.

The tasks in Part Four might be used in the professional development of teachers, both as a site for discussion of student work, as suggested by LeMahieu and Horton, and as a complex task for their own exploration, as suggested by Lappan and Cuevas. Because these tasks are more open-ended than most in previous sections, the mathematical analysis sections do not include complete solutions, but instead suggest some of the mathematical and pedagogical issues and some sources of data or other useful information. **Estimating Area** (p. 145) brings to light mathematical ideas such as the distinction between distance, area, and volume, scaling factors, and estimation, possibly leading to calculus ideas such as limit and integration. Like the tasks in Part Three, this is a task that may be fruitfully revisited several times in a student's career.

Timing Traffic Lights (p. 147) concerns a workplace situation usually considered by town and city planners. The ideas are similar to the ideas behind scheduling trains, airplanes, and canal-boats. The potential interest for students is that city planners' solutions (both the good and the bad) can be seen in everyday life. This task may be used to explore mathematical ideas such as distance, rate, time, velocity, modeling, and representation.

Buying a Used Car (p. 153) is an everyday situation about which people do not often think mathematically. Yet, by considering in the analysis not only estimates of the purchase price and repair costs but also insurance, taxes, depreciation, interest on a loan, and inflation, there is high potential for rich mathematical discussion.

REFERENCE

National Council of Teachers of Mathematics. (1991). *Professional standards for teaching mathematics*. Reston, VA: Author.

13 PEDAGOGICAL IMPLICATIONS FOR PROBLEM-CENTERED TEACHING

GLENDA T. LAPPAN
MICHIGAN STATE UNIVERSITY

No other decision that teachers make has a greater impact on students' opportunity to learn and on their perceptions about what mathematics is than the selection or creation of the tasks with which the teacher engages the students in studying mathematics. Here the teacher is the architect, the designer of the curriculum:

> The activity in which knowledge is developed and deployed . . . is not separate from or ancillary to learning and cognition. Nor is it neutral. Rather, it is an integral part of what is learned. Situations might be said to co-produce knowledge through activity. (Brown, Collins, & Duguid, 1989)

In order to develop productive notions about mathematics, students must have opportunities to be actually involved in doing mathematics—to explore interesting situations that can in some way be mathematicized; to look for patterns; to make conjectures; to look for evidence to support their conjectures; to make logical arguments for their conjectures; to make predictions or reach conclusions supported by evidence; to invent new ways to use their mathematical knowledge and tools to solve problems; and to abstract from experiences with solving problems the common mathematical concepts, ideas, skills, procedures, and structures that have more universal application.

In selecting a mathematical task, a teacher judges how well the task represents the embedded concepts and procedures that are the goals of instruction, how likely the students are to bump into the mathematics in the course of investigating the task, how well the task represents what is entailed in doing mathematics, and what skill development the task will or can support. An experienced teacher asks the question, "With what mathematics does the task surround the students?" Teachers also have to balance their selection of mathematical tasks to include tasks that allow and promote the usefulness of mathematics in solving authentic problems with all of their inherent messiness.

Here is an example of such a task. Consider the data in Table 13-1, taken from an advertisement in a Florida newspaper.

TABLE 13-1: Monthly charges for various Internet access providers			
ACCESS PROVIDER	MONTHLY RATE	HOURS INCLUDED	COST OF ADDITIONAL HOURS
TDO Online	$24.94	100	$2.00
America Online	$9.95	5	$2.95
CompuServe (Basic)	$9.95	5	$2.95
CompuServe (Super Value)	$24.95	20	$1.95
Prodigy (Basic)	$9.95	5	$2.95
Prodigy (30/30)	$30.00	30	$2.95

Suppose you are in the market for an Internet access provider. Which of the services in the table would be the best option for you to choose? The answer to this question is, "It depends!" One way to approach the problem would be to build tables and form graphical representations of each plan for different number of hours of use. Creating representations that allow comparisons is desirable. Tools such as graphing calculators or spreadsheets could be used. The solution is, of course, not a resounding endorsement for one of the services, but a more serious analysis of what ifs; an analysis that shows which plan is optimal when a desired number of hours of access is specified.

If teachers make the decision to use such a task in their classrooms, they have the responsibility to determine its mathematical potential. What mathematics can students learn from analyzing this situation? What mathematics are they most likely to use? Each of the plans can be represented by a piecewise linear relationship between cost and hours of use. This engages students in identifying variables and writing equations describing relationships that are constant for a number of hours and that change in a predictable fashion after that time. This is the essence of mathematical modeling. After modeling the situation with equations, tables of values, or graphs, students have to analyze the representation to make comparisons. They are likely to have to find points of intersection for the relationships. They may look at rates of change or slopes of lines. The important thing is that the task is rich with important, useful, connected, applicable mathematics.

TEACHING THROUGH BIGGER PROBLEMS

While the payoff for students can be very great, teaching through big problems increases the complexity of classroom instruction for teachers who are often imbued with the traditional view that mathematics is a well-ordered sequence of rules and procedures, mostly concerned with numbers and number operations. Many prospective and some practicing teachers do not expect mathematics to make sense, but they do expect to be able to remember a rule from which a solution can be swiftly found. They view the role of the teacher as explaining how to do the tasks and telling students when they are correct. Teachers with the traditional view can teach traditional classes confidently if they know the rules, the procedures, and when to apply them. Unless the teacher's mathematical understanding is deep and connected, however, such an approach often misses opportunities to make connections with other mathematics and with student thinking.

It takes a great deal of effort, and time, to create a new vision of what mathematics learning could be. Experience in working on "big problems" helps change how preservice teachers see themselves as learners of mathematics. "We were trained for so many years," reported Tamara, an older woman with weak mathematical background. "This is the way you do it. It becomes a way of thinking. This was the way I had always done mathematics so I've had to totally reorient myself. You have to restructure your whole way of thinking about mathematics and that alone is a big job. . . . To know mathematics means being able to say, 'this would make sense.' To know why something works and to be able to express it, you have to be able to communicate it. . . . You have to experience math, interact with it. You have to struggle to put things together and take them apart. If something doesn't work, you just try something else. . . . You need to experience it and talk about it, not just memorize it." (Schram, 1992, pp. 26, 34)

Another prospective teacher, Kim, struggled throughout the first two courses in her program. In her later courses, she began to gain confidence in her ability to think about the problems posed. "Math 201 was the hardest of the courses in the sequence because I really struggled with trying to think about math differently. . . . Now I am willing to continue working on a problem for a long time. Before, just forget it, if I didn't know the answer when I looked at a problem. I didn't even try further." (Schram, 1992, p. 32)

Preservice and inservice teachers who work on big problems become more willing to persevere with them. They develop mathematical resources, both intellectual and personal, that give them confidence in their ability to tackle real problems. They move from approaching mathematics as a technical subject to approaching mathematics as a sense-making enterprise based on careful observation, invention, making connections, gathering data, making conjectures, and seeking evidence.

Teachers face enormous complexities in attempting to create environments for learning mathematics in which students engage in making sense, individually and in groups, of big problems. Problem-centered teaching is demanding and requires of teachers an understanding of mathematics that will enable them to help students in their search to make sense of and use mathematics. Such instruction values students' thinking. Students are seen as "thinkers with emerging theories about the world" (Brooks & Brooks, 1993) rather than as passive recipients of information.

PROBLEM-CENTERED TEACHING

As the nature of the mathematical tasks changes, teachers must develop new classroom roles. If students are to have opportunities to explore rich problems within which mathematics will be confronted, teachers have to learn how to be effective in at least four new roles:

- Engaging students in the task;

- Pushing student thinking while the exploration is proceeding;

- Helping students to make the mathematics more explicit during whole-class and group interaction and synthesis;

- Using and responding to the diversity of the classroom to create an environment in which all students feel empowered to learn mathematics.

A reflective teacher realizes that engaging students in a task does not mean just having fun with its context. It is important, of course, for students to understand the context. But having an inclination to seek ways to mathematicize the situation they are exploring is critical. The teacher has to work with the students to help them understand which questions mathematics can help answer in the situation. This means keeping an eye on the mathematical goal in posing the task. This does not mean that the teacher structures the mathematical questions so that no thinking or work is left to the student. It means that the teacher keeps the focus on the big question embedded in the task and uses his or her judgment about whether this is a time when the students are to formulate questions for themselves or to find answers to problems in the situation that are posed by the situation or the teacher.

As the students work on the task posed—often in groups, always using tools such as calculators, computers, and physical manipulatives, as well as intellectual tools such as analogies—the teacher can assess what sense the students are making of the task and of the mathematics. By circulating among groups of students the instructor can ask students for evidence to support their conjectures and can redirect groups that are off-task or floundering. Here the teacher is a coach, a guide, an interlocutor, and an assessor of student progress and problems.

After groups have made progress on the task, the teacher and the class can come together to look at the different answers, to examine the data collected, to look at the strategies used, to examine the conjectures the groups have made and their supporting evidence, and to look at the proposed solutions and the reasoning to support the conclusions reached. It is during group sense-making that the teacher must be alert to the mathematical goals embedded in the task—to bring the mathematics alive, to help students make it more explicit and powerful, and to help students connect what they have learned to things they already know. This is where the teacher can work most effectively to set high expectations, both for students' mathematical performance and for the ways in which students engage in discussions with each other.

For teachers, it is daunting to examine what they need to know in order to help develop mathematical power for all students. Few teachers know enough to feel comfortable with this type of self-examination. However, a first step is to recognize that we all have things to learn. As students often learn most effectively in groups, so teachers will find that learning alone is unlikely to be as powerful as engaging in dialogue with other teachers. In order to get started, teachers need motivation for engaging in a daily search for tasks, materials, questions, and responses that will enable students to learn. Teachers have to focus on what students are learning rather than on simply "covering" the curriculum. Part of this has to do with the professionalism of teachers. Being professional includes managing the dilemmas of teaching in a thoughtful way, constantly trying to get smarter about the possibilities.

REFERENCES

Brooks, J. G. & Brooks, M. G. (1993). *The case for constructivist classrooms*. Alexandria, VA: Association for Supervision and Curriculum Development.

Brown, J. S., Collins, A., & Duguid, P. (1989). Situated cognition and the culture of learning. *Educational Researcher, 18*(1), 32-42.

Schram, P. (1992). *Learning mathematics to teach: What students learn about mathematical content and reasoning in a conceptually oriented course*. Unpublished doctoral dissertation, Michigan State University, East Lansing.

GLENDA T. LAPPAN is a Professor in the Department of Mathematics at Michigan State University. Her research interests are in the related areas of teaching and learning mathematics and supporting teachers to improve their practice. She is currently Vice Chair of the Mathematical Sciences Education Board and is President of the National Council of Teachers of Mathematics (NCTM), 1998-2000. She is Co-Director of the National Science Foundation funded Connected Mathematics Project and a member of the National Education Research Policy and Priorities Board. She chaired the development of the grades 5-8 part of the NCTM *Curriculum and Evaluation Standards for School Mathematics* and was the overall Chair for the development of the NCTM *Professional Standards for Teaching Mathematics*.

14 The Role of Complex Mathematical Tasks in Teacher Education

Gilbert J. Cuevas
University of Miami

The NCTM *Curriculum and Evaluation Standards* promotes increased emphasis on problem solving, mathematical communication, thinking, and reasoning. The resulting gap between a "traditional" and a reform-based approach to mathematics instruction poses a challenge for teacher educators as they develop strategies to help both preservice and classroom teachers implement the *Standards*. To help teachers become thoroughly familiar with the kinds of instructional activities that reflect the *Standards*, mathematics educators in teacher preparation programs can focus on processes similar to those recommended for students. The use of complex mathematical tasks can play a very important role in closing the gap between what teachers have traditionally done in the mathematics classroom and the approaches emphasized in the *Standards*.

A primary purpose of such tasks is to engage students in meaningful and worthwhile activities that lead to understanding of mathematics as a subject matter that has real-life applications. Complex mathematical tasks have several noteworthy aspects. First, they can be thought of as instructional activities that focus on specific sets of ideas and skills. Second, they demand active involvement by both students and teachers. Finally, such tasks should provide opportunities for expansion and reinforcement of learning. This learning should focus on the exploration of concepts being addressed in class, on the reinforcement of skills and ideas, on connections between ideas, and on the promotion of student communication through discussion, justification of solutions, and explanations of mathematical processes.

My personal experience in teaching mathematics methods courses has convinced me that the use of complex tasks helps teachers become oriented toward a *Standards*-based approach. Such tasks encourage classroom teachers to explore instructional strategies that reflect a problem-solving approach to mathematics education. In addition, they help teachers to see the value of classroom discourse for student learning and also to develop strategies that will assist students in improving their communication skills. Just as students need time to acquire the knowledge, strategies, and skills needed to deal effectively with tasks at different levels of complexity, teachers also need opportunities to develop a mental picture of how such tasks can be integrated into typical classroom activities.

Teachers who have limited experience with complex tasks regularly raise certain questions primarily concerning their desire to know how to implement these instructional activities in their classrooms effectively and how to help students get the most out of the experiences. Teachers ask questions such as the following:

- How can I know if the level of the mathematics addressed by the task is too difficult for my students?

- How can I help my students see that a task may be approached in more than one way?

- In what ways can I incorporate complex tasks into the curriculum that I am supposed to teach?

- How do I grade students on this?

- How do I make sure that all the skills and concepts in the curriculum are addressed?

Other questions have focused on helping students learn from the tasks:

- How do I know that the approaches the students have used are appropriate and lead to correct solutions?

- How do I provide feedback to students on their performance?

- What do I do if students cannot begin the task or are not able to describe what they have done, to draw conclusions, or to justify their solutions?

In the search for the answers to these questions I have found five guiding principles for the preparation of teachers. They are as follows.

Model a problem-oriented classroom environment. In methods courses for preservice teachers, complex tasks and "big problems" can be used throughout. They can be integrated into classroom activities to begin the study of particular mathematical topics. For example, the following task introduces the number concept:

> Suppose a friend told you she had a suitcase large enough to hold one million one-dollar bills. She asked you to help her bring the suitcase to a bank. Could you lift such a suitcase?

Complex tasks also can be used to summarize and reinforce ideas and concepts dealt with at different times during the course. Some tasks are used for assessment purposes. Preservice students work in small groups on these tasks and, upon completion, present their solutions to the class. Members of the class provide the group with evaluation feedback through the use of a predetermined rubric.

Provide experiences with tasks at all levels of mathematical complexity. Some secondary students will find certain tasks difficult for reasons ranging from inexperience with the activities involved to lack of appropriate mathematical background. Teachers should develop strategies to identify tasks that provide a challenge to students without being impossible to complete. Such strategies and sensitivity to the level of task difficulty can be acquired through exposure to a variety of mathematical tasks of different levels of complexity. Preservice as well as classroom teachers need to have numerous opportunities to engage in mathematical tasks, to analyze their mathematical content, and to develop solution strategies. Throughout these experiences, teachers must be guided to develop a framework by which they make decisions about the mathematical content of a task and its difficulty level. I have found that this is best accomplished when teachers reflect on and discuss the tasks.

Promote discussion of mathematical tasks, their content, and solutions. I have found three successful approaches to promote classroom discourse: small-group exploration and discussion of a given task, individual or group presentations of solutions to the whole class, and class discussion of students' approaches and solutions to tasks. For the latter, I present the class with samples of student work that I have collected in the local schools. The preservice teachers first analyze the work individually, then discuss it in small groups, and, finally, present their comments to the whole class. These experiences provide teachers with opportunities to explore a variety of student approaches to the tasks—some more effective than others—and to identify errors in mathematics or reasoning. Also, these exercises allow teachers to construct feedback as if they were communicating with the students whose work was examined.

Emphasize development of communication skills. Communication skills and the promotion of classroom discourse in mathematics should be approached developmentally. We cannot assume that if we give students an unstructured task such as "use data from current newspaper advertisements to examine the economics of buying a car versus leasing" that they will give complete explanations of procedures, solutions, and conclusions. Teachers should guide students in the development of mathematical communication until students achieve the skills and comfort level to communicate mathematical ideas effectively. A teacher using the buying versus leasing task might structure communication with a framework such as the following:

- Describe the facts stated in the newspaper advertisements.

- Describe the differences and similarities in the facts among these advertisements.

- Describe the factors you need to take into account to begin your comparison of buying versus leasing.

- Describe how you decide whether it is more economical to buy or lease a car.

- Write your conclusions and your reasons that support your conclusions.

Provide opportunities for reflection about the tasks and their implementation with students. Teachers need time to reflect on the mathematical content, thinking and reasoning requirements, student solutions, and communication demands of each task. In this way, teachers will develop strategies to address the concerns posed earlier in this essay. In methods courses, I require students to write reflections about tasks they have completed. These reflections are then shared in small groups during class time. In workshops, I give participants opportunities to reflect on task features and possible implementation strategies.

Rather than concluding with a personal thought on the role of complex mathematical tasks in teacher education, I will share a comment made by a teacher on this matter: "By working through the tasks, I became confident of my mathematical ability, developed ideas for using them with students, and I am now more sensitive to the difficulties and obstacles students may have in their learning of mathematics."

GILBERT J. CUEVAS is a Professor of Mathematics Education in the School of Education at the University of Miami. He has directed a number of professional teacher development projects in bilingual, mathematics, and science education. He has also served as a member of the Mathematical Sciences Education Board.

15 Assessment Conversations as a Tool for Reform

PAUL G. LEMAHIEU
UNIVERSITY OF DELAWARE AND DELAWARE DEPARTMENT OF EDUCATION

MARSHÁ T. HORTON
DELAWARE DEPARTMENT OF EDUCATION

What role might extended, open-ended tasks play in assessment? Through the good efforts of many individuals and the reform of large-scale assessment initiatives, we have begun to ask such questions. While there is yet much to be done to bring technical quality and intellectual rigor to this particular aspect of a more general reform movement, it is clear that we will never again think of assessment in precisely the same terms as those that have dominated our thinking for the past century or more. What is less certain is what role assessment should play in order to maximize its contribution to broader reform efforts.

Some see assessment as an agent of reform, as a lever that, when properly applied, lifts the system (and the individuals within it) to improved performance by increasing accountability. This view is based on a well-established logic about the force and influence of assessment and accountability: clear articulation of goals will make public the expectations for individuals and the education system; appropriate and adequate assessments will reveal the performance of individuals, schools, and systems; and appropriate sanctions and rewards will provide the motivation to improve effectiveness and productivity.

This "lever view" is plausible and quite possible. We are not too optimistic, however, about assessments (reformed or otherwise) used solely in this way and detect an underlying cynical assumption: that those who work in our schools have the skills and the capacities to help their students learn better, but for some reason choose not to do so. Our experience within schools does not support this cynical view. We have encountered some who (sad to say) lack the requisite familiarity with national, state, or local standards for student learning; more who have not had the opportunity to develop or refine the skills necessary to ensure their students' success; and still more who are constrained by a lack of intellectual or material support from their school districts or systems for the kinds of practice necessary to prefigure accomplishment of the standards. We have not encountered many who willfully choose not to perform well.

However, tasks like the ones in this volume, if we assume that these are assessment tasks, do offer a potentially powerful but very different role for assessment in reform. They might play an "instrumental" role, in which teachers work with such tasks in a variety of ways that challenge their practice. First and most obvious is the signaling function, helping to make the standards concrete. This is particularly important as the concepts (curricular and instructional) underlying the standards become more complex and more subtle.

There is a second instrumental use for tasks like those documented here, also related to teachers' growth and development. Such tasks can be strategically used to stimulate and discipline what we have come to term the "assessment conversation." Making these tasks (as well as the student work that they elicit) central to professional discourse can challenge teachers' notions of students' capacities. Appropriate professional development focused on the use of these tasks can powerfully shape teachers' notions about what constitutes high-quality student work and what serves as adequate evidence of such quality. Our experience with the instrumental use of tasks like these is instructive: assessment and the development and use of tasks such as these can be approached so as to maximize the beneficial impact on instructional practice.

Just as standards-based reform requires so much more by way of professional judgment, there is a need to warrant that judgment. Given the very complex systems within which educational professionals work, faith and trust must be located somewhere. That confidence can be placed in the people who work within the system or can be placed in mechanisms designed to control people and their behaviors. The current reform movement places faith in people rather than mechanisms. Whether one considers local democratization and site-based management; teacher empowerment and shared-decision making; the increased role of teachers in curriculum definition and selection; efforts at organizational development founded upon continuous improvement and learning community ideals; or the advent of assessment approaches that more explicitly privilege human judgment—in all of these cases the trust and the hopes for a high-performing system are vested in the teachers and other professionals who serve within it.

However, the call for placing our trust in the empowerment of professionals requires that serious action be taken to warrant that trust. This is the basis for the persistent urging for investment in capacity building at the system level and in the professional development of individuals. As part of that professional development, we are optimistic about the potential of well-designed "assessment conversations" as instruments to shape teachers' expectations, beliefs, and practices.

Assessment systems offer important opportunities to show that our trust in teachers is warranted and thereby facilitate beneficial change. Well constructed assessment activities and the efforts to employ them strategically in professional development activity permit teachers to engage in review of student work; develop shared notions of high-quality student performance; determine what constitutes adequate evidence of high quality; and ultimately to reflect upon the kinds of learning experiences that challenge traditional practice and produce the desired performances.

We see immense potential for the use of tasks, such as those in this volume, as assessments within a process of ongoing and sustained development designed to support professional growth. We have done so involving large numbers of teachers who meet regularly (at least monthly for up to two days at a time) over an extended period (two years) to develop assessment tasks and to pilot and refine them in their classrooms. In these assessment-development conversations, teachers share and closely examine students' work. A professional discourse is provoked by the simple guiding question, "What can we tell about this student as a learner in mathematics?"

The ensuing discussions are closely documented and analyzed for "points of evaluative judgment." These points of judgment represent the beginnings of a framework or rubric for evaluating student work. Over time, insights grow in number, depth, and sophistication, and are synthesized into a framework that teachers use and refine.

Can an evaluative framework derived from one collection of student work be applied meaningfully to others? Will it hold up across a diverse array of students (with respect to abilities, levels of performance, cultural and linguistic backgrounds, gender, etc.)? Can it be applied with discipline and consistency (yet insight and sophistication) by many teachers? These and similar questions are addressed by taking the evaluative framework and applying it to new and broader collections of student work. At the same time that an evaluative perspective is being validated in this way, the sophistication, consistency, and reliability of shared interpretations are also being refined. Over time, these conversations, begun with a group of teachers involved in assessment development, are replicated in professional development activities on a broader and more extensive scale.

In our experience, two things have invariably been realized through these "assessment conversations." First, all who participate in them leave with higher and more clearly articulated aspirations for student performance. This should not be the least surprising, as the derivation of criteria and expectations for quality in mathematical performances is essentially additive. One teacher sees certain things in a piece of student work, while the next recognizes some (but perhaps not all) of them and adds others. These assessment conversations proceed until the final set of aspirations (criteria of quality) are far greater than the initial one or that of any one teacher at the outset. Simply put, these assessment conversations increase the expectations of all those who participate in them.

The second effect of these assessment conversations is that a shared framework for interpreting and evaluating student work emerges. The aspirations and expectations associated with this framework become commonly understood by the teachers and more consistently applied to all their students. Again, the nature of these conversations (long-term shared encounters and reflections) supports this outcome.

These two outcomes of assessment conversations—elevated aspirations and more consistently held and applied aspirations—are key ingredients in a recipe for beneficial change. Educational research is nowhere more compelling than in its documentation of the relationship between expectations and student performance. Where expectations are high and represent demanding yet attainable goals, students strive to respond and, ultimately, they do achieve. Assessment conversations, focused upon tasks such as those in this volume and student work produced in response to them, provide a powerful device through which to warrant investment in the human side of the educational system. It is when assessment is used to provoke conversations of this kind that we find cause for optimism about the role of assessment in reform.

PAUL G. LEMAHIEU currently serves as Director of the Delaware Education Research and Development Center and as Associate Professor of Educational Studies at the University of Delaware. He is currently the principal investigator of Delaware's Statewide Systemic Initiative for Mathematics and Science Reform. He also holds a senior staff appointment in the Delaware Department of Education as Special Undersecretary of Education for Policy Research and Development. LeMahieu has received a number of major awards for his contributions to educational theory and practice from the American Educational Research Association, the Evaluation Research Society, the Buros Institute of Measurement, the National Association of Test Directors, and the Association for Supervision and Curriculum Development. He is a former member of the Mathematical Sciences Education Board, having served on its Executive Committee and as Chair of its National Forum on School Mathematics.

MARSHÁ T. HORTON is the Associate State Superintendent of Assessments and Accountability for the Delaware Department of Education. In this position, Horton coordinates the design and implementation of the Delaware State Testing Program and coordinates the department's teacher certification and licensure responsibilities. She has served on the National Reading Research Center National Advisory Board, the Sweet Briar College Board of Directors, and the New Standards Project Literacy Advisory Panel. She recently co-authored a paper with Dr. Paul LeMahieu on standards-based accountability and has served as a consultant to many school districts and national organizations.

ESTIMATING AREA

TASK. In medicine, calculation of body surface area is sometimes very important. For example, severe burns are usually described as covering a percentage of the body surface area. Some chemotherapy drug dosages are based on body surface area. How might body surface area be measured? What factors influence the accuracy of the estimates?

COMMENTARY. Three main mathematical themes could be emphasized in this task: estimation, partitioning, and successive approximation. These need to be combined with an understanding of the relationships among measurements of distance, area, volume, and weight. This task might also be used as an introduction to the calculus topic of integration.

In everyday life, we estimate area in order to determine how much paint to use in painting our homes, how much carpet to buy for a room, how many plants to buy for a garden, or how much grass seed or fertilizer to buy for our lawns. Some approaches to this task can also lead to discussion of proportion and scale. Highway designers, landscape designers, interior designers, and architects all make and interpret diagrams drawn to scale.

An important component of this task is estimating the error in measurement—perhaps finding both upper and lower bounds, which lays some of the groundwork for calculus. In some cases, upper and lower bounds may lend themselves to further refinement.

MATHEMATICAL ANALYSIS. There are many possible avenues of approach for this task. One possibility is to consider the human body as a collection of cylinders. Each limb, the head, and the midsection, for example, might be approximated as cylinders. Finding the sum of the lateral surface area of each of these would give a good first approximation. This procedure could be refined by adding the areas of the "ends" of the cylinders and subtracting the areas where the cylinders are attached together. The procedure could be further refined by considering, for example, the head and the neck to be a sphere and a cylinder, respectively, and eventually by approximating the fingers as individual cylinders.

A very different approach would be to take pictures of a person—front, lateral, and top views—and to superimpose a flat grid on the pictures to approximate the surface area. This approach would require additional discussion of proportions due to the scale of the picture. The accuracy would depend not only on the size of the grid relative to the dimensions of the person in the picture, but also on the reasonableness of projecting a three-dimensional human onto two-dimensional pictures to estimate surface area. Using smaller and smaller grids to achieve successively better approximations foreshadows some of the ideas of calculus.

An approach that also foreshadows calculus but doesn't involve scaling is to cover the body with patches of cloth of known area. If the pieces of cloth are all the same size, the accuracy of the approximation would depend on the size of the pieces. Covering the body with cloth suggests a very elegant approach that doesn't involve calculus at all. If the entire body is clothed with close-fitting, non-stretch cloth of consistent thickness and density, the surface area may be determined by weighing the cloth and then dividing by the weight of a piece of cloth of unit area.

From any of the above approximations, students would be afforded experience and data from which to discuss the adequacy of the standard medical practice of approximating surface area by using the following formula:

$$\sqrt{\frac{Height \times Weight}{3600}}$$

where height is measured in centimeters and weight is measured in kilograms. The result of the calculation gives an approximation for body surface area in square meters. Thus, for example, a person who is 5'10" (177.8 cm) tall and weighs 180 lbs. (81.8 kg) has a surface area of approximately $\sqrt{177.8 \times 81.8/3600} \approx$ 2 square meters. This calculation is based in part on the assumption that, for humans, weight is roughly proportional to volume, an assumption that is also worthy of investigation. The formula has a certain dimensional consistency in that the product of height (one-dimensional) and weight (three-dimensional) gives a four dimensional quantity. Taking the square root then gives a two-dimensional result, consistent with the fact that surface area is a two-dimensional quantity.

EXTENSIONS. Given a map of the United States, students might estimate the area in square miles of the states of Colorado, Texas, Florida, and Vermont and compare their estimates to the actual area of each state given in an almanac or an encyclopedia. The students might discuss the accuracy of their estimates and why the process is easier for some states than for others. If the students are using a square grid to do the approximation, they can ask: What size grid is needed to estimate the area to a given accuracy?

Using a map causes another kind of measurement error. Because a map is a flat representation of the curved surface of the earth, there is some inevitable error in the way it shows angles or areas. How big an area on the earth must be considered before such errors are measurable? Understanding the reason for this distortion and some of the projections used by map makers involves solid geometry and spherical trigonometry.

Students also could explore the extent to which a state's topography affects its surface area. Is the surface area of a 100-mile square section of western Colorado the same as a 100-mile square section of eastern Colorado? This leads to interesting questions about how surveyors actually calculate the area of steeply sloped land.

Other extensions might concern volume or perimeter, estimating, for instance, the amount of air in a school building to determine how often the ventilation system refreshes the air. Approximating the perimeter of a territory can lead to some interesting findings. When the coastline of Britain on a geographical map is approximated by line segments corresponding to 500 km on the map, the result is 2600 km. When the coastline is approximated by segments corresponding to 17 km, the result is 8640 km—more than a three-fold increase. In contrast, when the border of Utah is measured in the same ways, the estimated length goes from 1450 km to about 1890 km—not even a two-fold increase. Fractal dimension is concerned with characterizing differences like these (Peitgen et al., 1992).

REFERENCE

Peitgen, H.-O. et al. (1992). *Fractals for the classroom.* New York: Springer-Verlag.

TIMING TRAFFIC LIGHTS

TASK. A stretch of a suburban road lined with shopping plazas carries heavy commuter traffic. The road has 15 traffic signals, unevenly spaced, at the intersections with cross streets and mall entrances. Figure out how to time the lights in order to maximize the flow of commuter traffic.

COMMENTARY. One approach to this task uses a very powerful geometric technique to model the situation. The technique combines the information for cars (given by two-dimensional position versus time graphs) with the information given for traffic lights (given by one-dimensional time graphs showing how long they are red, green, and yellow). Similar diagrams are used in the planning of highways, railroad schedules, and canals. This task and the techniques in the solution below provide opportunities for geometric thinking, reasoning from graphs, and connections between slope and velocity.

MATHEMATICAL ANALYSIS. Rather than a complete solution, which would require precise data about placement of lights and about typical traffic flow and consideration of many alternatives, this section discusses a solution for a simple case. This simple case can provide understanding of the geometric model and insights into the general case.[1]

Suppose the road travels north-south and has only three lights. Label the lights A, B, and C, and suppose that lights B and C are 0.25 and 0.38 miles north of light A, respectively. First consider only light A. Suppose that it follows a 1-minute cycle—green for 30 seconds, yellow for 5 seconds, and red for 25 seconds. The pattern of the light can be represented graphically on a line (Figure 1).

To show the position of cars over time, the distance from light A may be represented on a vertical axis with time represented on a horizontal axis as in Figure 1. For smooth traffic flow, cars going a moderate speed should be able to go through all three lights without stopping. Consider first only cars traveling north and assume that all cars travel at a constant speed of 30 mph. Figure 2 shows possible positions of 12 north-bound cars over the first 120 seconds after the beginning of a cycle of light A. The first car goes through light A 5 seconds after it turns green and the sixth goes through at 30 seconds, just as the light turns yellow. The white space in the middle of the graph shows that light A, when it is red, causes "spaces" in the traffic flow, if traffic entering from other roads is ignored. In this representation, the slope of a line is equal to the speed of the car it represents. Here, the slopes are 0.5 miles/60 seconds, or 30 mph.

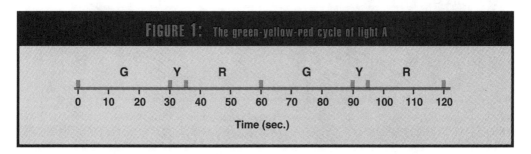

FIGURE 1: The green-yellow-red cycle of light A

```
      G        Y      R            G        Y      R
   |        |   |        |         |        |   |        |
   0  10  20  30  40  50  60  70  80  90  100  110  120
                        Time (sec.)
```

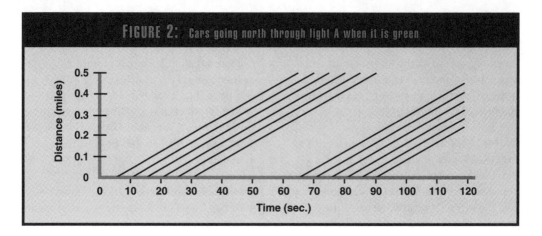

FIGURE 2: Cars going north through light A when it is green

The lines are parallel because all of the cars are assumed to be traveling at the same speed.

Lights B and C are represented as horizontal lines in Figure 3. The lines have been partially dotted to show "windows"—time intervals during which the light should be green to allow unimpeded flow of the 12 cars from Figure 2. Each light should turn green shortly before the first car arrives at the light so that the car will not need to slow down before reaching the light. The diagram shows that light B should be green from about 30 until 60 seconds and again from 90 until 120 seconds. Allowing for a 5-second yellow light, this implies a 25-second red light between the green intervals. Thus, light B should follow the same cycle as light A, but the cycle is shifted in phase by 30 seconds. Light C should be green between about 45 and 75 seconds and then again at 105 seconds. Thus, this light should also follow the same cycle, but phase shifted by 45 seconds.

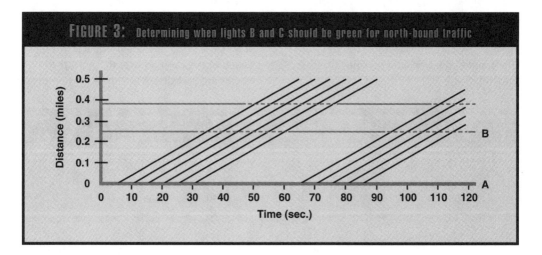

FIGURE 3: Determining when lights B and C should be green for north-bound traffic

This is a sufficient one-directional solution for three lights. In fact, with this sort of phase-shifting of the same light pattern, any number of lights could be added to this road and still allow for unimpeded flow of traffic in the north-bound direction. Lights on one-way streets are often timed in a manner similar to this, although the expected speed may be different from the 30 mph used here.

Allowing for similarly smooth flow of traffic in two directions is much more difficult. Figure 4 shows both north-bound traffic as in Figure 2 and also some south-bound traffic that would go through light A when it is green. Note that if light B uses the same green intervals as in Figure 3, it will allow both north- and south-bound traffic to flow unimpeded. In order to allow all the north- and south-bound traffic to flow through light C, however, it must be green all the time, which would not be practical.

One solution to this dilemma is to give priority to the north-bound traffic and time the lights as indicated in Figure 3. Then north-bound traffic can flow unimpeded, but the south-bound traffic will always have to stop at at least one of the lights. Alternatively, priority could be given to the south-bound traffic.

Another approach is to change the period of the light cycles. If the lights are on a 90-second rather than a 60-second cycle, then light C can be timed to accommodate both north- and south-bound traffic, as shown in Figure 5. Now, however, light B needs an excessively long green interval to accommodate both directions of traffic.

Neither a 60-second light cycle (Figure 4) nor a 90-second light cycle (Figure 5) can accommodate traffic in both directions at both lights B and C. Figures 4 and 5 do, however, suggest a compromise: a 75-second light cycle.

Figure 6 shows that with a 75 second light cycle, if both lights B and C are green from about 30 to about 75 seconds after the beginning of light A's cycle, most of the north- and south-bound traffic will flow unimpeded.

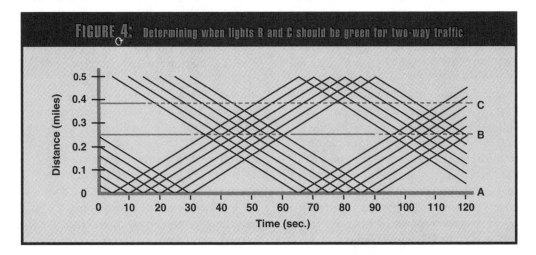

FIGURE 4: Determining when lights B and C should be green for two-way traffic

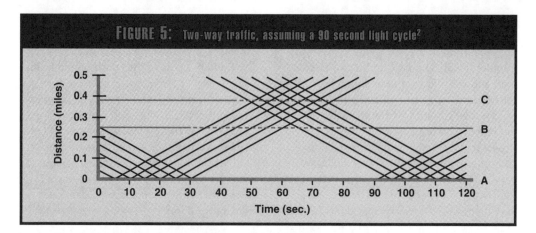

FIGURE 5: Two-way traffic, assuming a 90 second light cycle[2]

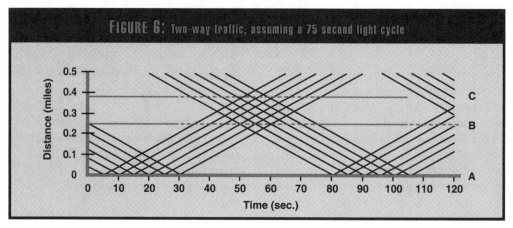

FIGURE 6: Two-way traffic, assuming a 75 second light cycle

EXTENSIONS. The discussion and diagrams above suggest that when there are only two lights or when the lights are evenly spaced, the light cycle may be adjusted to accommodate good traffic flow in both directions. When there are more than two lights and they are unevenly spaced, however, it is not always possible to allow for stop-free traffic in both directions on a two-way road. Is it possible to ensure that all cars stop at at most one of three lights? Some drivers get frustrated when they must stop at two or more consecutive lights. On a road with many unevenly spaced lights is it always possible to time the lights so this won't happen? On some two-way streets, five or more consecutive lights change as a group, allowing for most cars to pass through all the lights in the group without stopping. How does this approach compare to more flexible optimization?

The above discussion has not taken into account the east-west traffic. How should these requirements be factored in? If some of the east-west roads are major roads with much traffic, these requirements should be considered in any decisions about timing the lights. On the other hand, if they are minor roads, it is probably safe to assume that traffic from these roads will not benefit from long red signals on the north-south road.

The discussion above began with positions of the lights and tried to find a reasonable way to time the lights for traffic going 30 mph. What about the reverse? Given the timing of some traffic lights, what are the speeds that must be traveled so that cars do not have to stop? As shown in Figure 7, cars can be given positions by tilting the lines to fit the "windows" represented by green lights. The trick is to find slopes that correspond to appropriate driving speeds.

Under the scenario represented by the solid line in Figure 7, it takes the car 60 seconds to travel from light A to light B. If B – A represents the distance between the two lights, then the speed is (B – A)/60 feet per second (fps). If the distance between A and B is 2400 feet, then the speed is 40 fps, which is about 27 mph, and that's fine. But suppose the distance between A and B is 6000 feet. Then the speed would be 100 fps, or about

70 mph, and that's not sensible. In this case, the dotted line in Figure 7 might represent a more realistic possibility. Passing through the second "window" in the line representing light B corresponds to allowing two cycles of the lights to get from A to B. This doubles the time that it takes for the car to travel from light A to light B and cuts the speed in half to about 35 mph, which might be acceptable. In general, if N is a positive integer representing a number of cycles of light B, then the speed will be $(B – A)/(60N)$ feet per second. Just pick N to get the speed into a sensible range.

What if the road carries heavy commuter traffic northbound in the mornings and southbound in the evenings? Would it make sense to have different timings of the lights for the different rush hours? Does it make sense in very heavy traffic to slow down the expected speed of travel? What needs to happen to the timing of the lights to accommodate the slower speeds?

Much of the discussion has aimed to allow cars to pass through many lights without

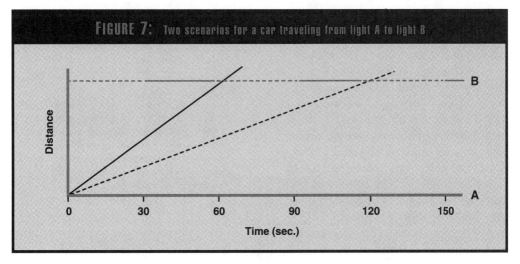

FIGURE 7: Two scenarios for a car traveling from light A to light B

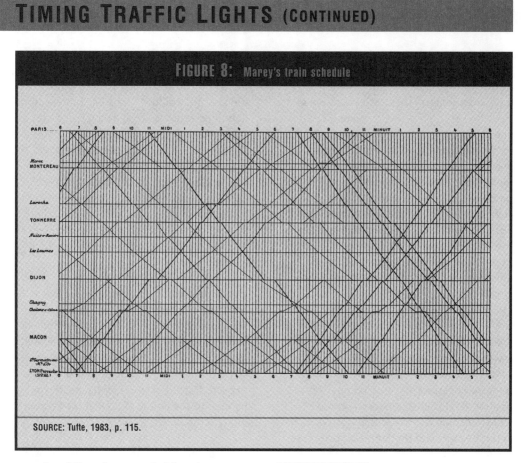

FIGURE 8: Marey's train schedule

SOURCE: Tufte, 1983, p. 115.

stopping. What about maximizing the capacity of the road? Will the solution be the same or different?

This sort of diagram is used in other situations, such as train scheduling (see Figure 8). For a one-track railroad line, or a canal like the Suez Canal which is one-way much of the way, you locate sidings (bypasses) on the distance axis where traffic in opposing directions can pass, and schedule trains (convoys) to get there at the right times. The planners of traffic for the Suez Canal use a similar diagram, but with the time and distance axes interchanged for historical reasons.

REFERENCES

Tufte, E. (1983). *The visual display of quantitative information*. Cheshire, CT: Graphics Press.

Walker, J. (1983). Amateur scientist: How to analyze a city traffic light system from the outside looking in. *Scientific American, 248*(3), 138-145.

NOTES

1. For other ideas and approaches, see Walker (1983).

2. A 90-second light cycle would likely include a longer green portion, allowing for more than 6 cars, at 5-second intervals, to pass through the green light. Nonetheless, Figure 5 includes only 6 cars through each cycle to allow for easier comparison with the other figures.

BUYING A USED CAR

TASK. How does the age of a used car affect its price? How does its age affect its repair costs? What is the best age at which to buy a used car?

COMMENTARY. Many people in the United States are dependent on cars, and students are no exception. This task may be particularly meaningful to students as they become consumers of cars.

Although this task begins with data collection, it leads quickly to other important mathematics, including graphs and scatterplots, linear regression, amortization, and optimization—to balance rising repair costs against falling purchase prices.

MATHEMATICAL ANALYSIS. Data for this task may be collected from consumer magazines, from car buying guides, or from the Internet. If data are gathered about prices and repair costs for used cars, they reveal opposite trends: newer cars tend to have lower repair costs, but older cars generally have lower purchase prices. Purchase price is a one-time cost, and repair costs are likely to be on-going. So to combine this information, students might first convert it to a common basis—either annual expenses (if the purchase price is paid out over time) or total costs (by adding up total expected repairs for the likely life of the car).

Once these data are combined, either in a spreadsheet or on a graph, it should be clear visually where the total costs are least. This

may be somewhere in the middle of the age or price range being examined, or it might be at one end or the other. For example, among cars older than ten years, it might be that the newest cars are the best buy because repair costs rise more rapidly than the drop in price as cars age.

Many people who are buying a used car may expect that their incomes will rise. In that case, they may not want to minimize the total cost but might be willing to bear larger repair expenses down the road in return for a lower purchase price.

EXTENSIONS. What is the relation between age and mileage? How much more value is there in a low-mileage car of a certain age? By collecting repair costs and plotting them by age and by mileage, it is possible to determine whether age or mileage is the better indicator of the reliability of the car. (Such data may be available—at least for specific brands—from the computerized repair records of automobile dealers.) Other extensions could look at differences between cars repaired at dealers' shops or at independent garages or in different regions of the country.

Another question a prospective car-buyer might want to consider is whether to buy or lease.

Finally, if the data are available, it would be interesting to find out how old a car needs to be before its price begins to rise—because it is becoming an antique.

Part Five

Epilogue

Epilogue

The introduction to *High School Mathematics at Work* begins by asserting that today's world provides rich and compelling examples of mathematical ideas in everyday and workplace settings. In short, workplace-based mathematics can be good mathematics for everyone. The volume goes on to explore opportunities and challenges posed by developments in the world outside of the classroom. Several points deserve mention and special emphasis. Because this document is part of a larger reform movement, some concerns must be addressed about the reform movement in general and also about the scope of the tasks in this volume. Once again, the tasks in this volume are not prescriptions for curriculum but examples that are intended to illuminate possibilities.

MATHEMATICS EDUCATION REFORM

At the heart of some of the recent concerns about K-12 education reform efforts are issues of subject matter content: scope, depth, and levels of conceptual reasoning and technical proficiency. Concerns have been raised, for example, that some proposed revisions of curricula omit important topics and place insufficient emphasis on technical proficiency to promote understanding. *High School Mathematics at Work* aims neither to broaden nor restrict the scope of the high school mathematics curriculum. Furthermore, technical proficiency and depth of content coverage are not necessarily reduced by inclusion of workplace and everyday applications of mathematics. To the contrary, such an approach can provide meaning that increases the depth of students' understanding as well as their levels of conceptual reasoning and technical proficiency. Of course, a necessary condition for such an outcome is that students have sufficient opportunity for mathematical closure—extracting and conceptualizing the mathematics underlying the problems.

THE SCOPE OF HIGH SCHOOL MATHEMATICS

By emphasizing connections between mathematics and workplace and everyday contexts, the mathematical content of this volume emphasizes some topics that have particularly striking, valuable, or widespread applications outside the classroom. Despite the broad range of tasks in this volume, statistics, discrete mathematics, and spatial reasoning receive little attention, and yet their relevance for today's world is without question. *High School Mathematics at Work* flags places in hospitals, banks, homes, and other familiar settings where important mathematical ideas are used. Many of these settings employ techniques which depend upon and lead to aspects of algebraic, geometric, and functional reasoning that have been and will always be recognized as crucial elements of a high school education.

A careful look at algebraic reasoning illustrates this point. Linear programming (a subset of algebra), for example, has many beautiful, important, and time-tested applications. That is why many textbooks already contain problems on this subject. More generally, algebraic reasoning is often addressed in *High School Mathematics at Work* through spreadsheets (rules for combining the entries of certain cells to produce the quantity that goes into another cell are just algebra in a new form). That some aspects of classical algebra do not appear more explicitly in *High School Mathematics at Work* should not be taken as a statement about their mathematical or practical value. Students heading to technical careers of any sort should understand how to use and interpret symbols. In fact, for all students, understanding of core algebraic skills and reasoning continues to be a key mathematical prerequisite.

Similar comments could be made about many other mathematical topics not explicitly mentioned in *High School Mathematics at Work*. Indeed, the Task Force for this volume identified quite a large number of mathematically important and delightful problems that were eventually not recommended for inclusion because their connection to workplace or everyday applications was less apparent than for others. Among the favorites not included were the following: calculating into how many regions n lines drawn at random divide the plane; and using probability calculations to see how the length of a play-off series affects the chances of the weaker team pulling off an upset by winning the series.

A Curriculum Is More Than Tasks

When one addresses concerns about reform-based materials as well as the fact that not all important high school mathematics is represented here, it is necessary once again to caution that the tasks in *High School Mathematics at Work* constitute neither a complete curriculum nor even student-ready curricular materials. All readers are welcome to see in these tasks potential for strengthening the mathematics education of all students, but no one should conclude that it is enough to teach these tasks or even a collection of exercises inspired by them. Any tasks need to be embedded in a coherent, well-developed mathematics curriculum that provides the mathematical understanding that a high school graduate should have. In the end, mathematics is "more than a toolbox," as Hugo Rossi recently put it. The act of abstraction is what makes it so powerful. After completing a series of workplace or everyday problems with students, we must always remember to help them understand that what we call mathematics comes from generalizing and organizing the common features among the solutions into a coherent structure. A quality mathematics curriculum is not crafted out of tasks alone but also depends upon how these tasks are knit together and what kinds of opportunities students are afforded for abstraction and deep conceptual development.

APPENDIXES

A

Sources of Problems and Tasks

Susan Forman and Lynn Arthur Steen

Potential tasks for *High School Mathematics at Work* were solicited from many sources. Printed announcements of the project were distributed at national meetings of various professional societies; e-mail invitations were sent to many mathematicians, educators, and policy leaders; special invitations were extended to leaders of major high school curriculum and assessment projects, both academic and vocational; panel presentations were arranged to address the key question of what mathematics every high school graduate should know and be able to do; and visits were made to corporations to solicit examples of typical work tasks that require mathematical knowledge and insight.

From this enormous volume and variety of problems, the Task Force and its consultants shaped tasks for inclusion in the volume—by selection, by revision, by combination, and by creation. Virtually none of the tasks presented here are the same as originally proposed: each has been transformed to fit the context of this volume. Similarly, teachers who may wish to use these or other tasks will need to adapt them to their own contexts. The process of adaptation reinforces one of the key lessons of *High School Mathematics at Work*, namely, that context is important for mathematics.

That said, we list below the types of sources we found helpful in preparing *High School Mathematics at Work*. Though this list is intended to be illustrative rather than exhaustive, we apologize for omitting any particularly fruitful sources. Similar lists tied to regional contexts should be of help to teachers who want to offer their students more locally relevant but similar tasks.

FROM INDUSTRY AND GOVERNMENT

Big companies and government agencies are awash in data, from the manufacturing floor to the sales office: effective companies expect all their employees to use these data for planning and quality control. For this project, we found interesting examples from different industrial and governmental sectors: transportation (Boeing), electronics (Motorola), entertainment (Disney), food (Starbucks), construction (Hilti), and health (Oregon Center for Health Statistics).

FROM SCHOOL-TO-WORK PROGRAMS

Many organizations are working to develop effective school-business partnerships. These programs operate under titles such as "tech-prep" and "school-to-work." They include regional education consortia (e.g., the East San Gabriel Valley Regional Occupational Project or the Pennsylvania Youth Apprenticeship Program), regional corporate consortia (e.g., the Washington State Manufacturing Technology Advisory Group or Craftsmanship 2000 in Tulsa, Oklahoma); and curriculum development organizations (e.g., the Consortium on Occupational Research and Development [CORD] in Waco, Texas, or the School-to-Work project of the Learning Research and Development Center [LRDC] at the University of Pittsburgh).

FROM HIGH SCHOOLS

Many districts have special high schools devoted to vocational or technological education. Some (e.g., Rindge School of Technical Arts in Cambridge, Massachusetts; Leander High School in Leander, Texas; the Williamson Free School of Mechanical Trades in Philadelphia) provide a comprehensive philosophy uniting vocational and academic education. Others (e.g., Franklin High School in Portland, Oregon, Brooklyn Technical High School in New York) have special projects (STELLA at Franklin, Design Challenge at Brooklyn Tech) that offer stimulating ideas for how mathematics relates to other subjects.

FROM COLLEGE PROGRAMS

Although *High School Mathematics at Work* is about high school mathematics, many programs with similar tasks can be found at two- and four- year colleges. Some of these have been supported by federal grants, others with local funds. Among those that contributed to *High School Mathematics at Work* are the Mathematics in Industry project at Henry Ford Community College, Dearborn, Michigan (Barbara Near, Project Director), Snapshots of Applications in Mathematics at SUNY College of Technology in Delhi, New York (Dennis Callas,

Project Director), and Interactive Mathematics at Mt. Hood Community College in Oregon (Penny Slingerland et al., project directors). More recent projects supported by the National Science Foundation's (NSF) Advanced Technological Initiative (ATE) program can be found at Wentworth Institute (Gary Simundza, Director) and Johns Hopkins University (Arnold Packer, Director).

FROM CURRICULUM AND ASSESSMENT PROJECTS

Many innovative tasks can be found in the material produced by the several nationally funded curriculum and assessment projects. *High School Mathematics at Work* benefited especially from ideas submitted by the Balanced Assessment Project, the Interactive Mathematics Project, the New Standards Project, and the Connecticut Academic Performance Test in Mathematics.

FROM INDIVIDUALS

Many individuals contributed special ideas to *High School Mathematics at Work*—far more than can be named here or even recalled. We do mention, however, a few individuals who direct centers or projects that we found to be particularly rich sources of ideas: Dick Stanley, Charles A. Dana Center, University of California, Berkeley; Peter Costa, Center for Applied Mathematics, University of St. Thomas; Avner Friedman, Director of the Institute for Mathematics and Its Applications at the University of Minnesota; Cindy Hannon, Tech Prep Coordinator, Maryland State Department of Education; Thomas Hsu, Cambridge Physics Outlet, Woburn, Massachusetts; and Martin Nahemow, Director of School-to-Work Programs, LRDC, University of Pittsburgh.

FROM COORDINATING ORGANIZATIONS

Several organizations serve as helpful sources of contacts for particular projects and programs. These include Schools that Work, a project directed by Gene Bottoms for the Southern Regional Education Board; the Advanced Technological Education (ATE) Program of the NSF (Elizabeth Teles and Gerhard Salinger, Program Directors); the National Center for Research in Vocational Education (NCRVE) at the University of California, Berkeley (Norton Grubb and David Stern, Directors); the Institute on Education and the Economy at Columbia University (Thomas Bailey, Director); and Jobs for the Future in Boston (Hilary Pennington, President and Susan Goldberger, Program Director).

FROM SPECIAL SOURCES

Ideas for tasks in *High School Mathematics at Work* also came from the National Security Agency's Summer Mathematics Teacher Institutes (Fort Meade, Maryland) and the TEAMS Competition of the Junior Engineering Technical Society (JETS). For similar problems from new sources, we suggest some of the NSF ATE projects, for example, the Sinclair Center and the Center for Image Processing in Education. Of course, some of the very best sources are the members of the Task Force for *High School Mathematics at Work*, who worked extensively with the many tasks that were reviewed in the process of preparing this volume.

These diverse institutions and programs illustrate both the particular sources from which *High School Mathematics at Work* was developed, and also the enormous variety of places that educators should look to in their search for tasks that are mathematically rich and contextually relevant.

B TASK FORCE MEMBERS

HYMAN BASS is Professor of Mathematics at Columbia University. He is Chair of the Mathematical Sciences Education Board (MSEB), has served on the Executive Committee for the American Mathematical Society, and was Chair of the Board of Trustees for the Mathematical Sciences Research Institute, Berkeley. He is a member of the National Academy of Sciences.

BRUCE JACOBS taught at Laney College in the Peralta Community College District for 24 years. During that time, he served as Director of the Experimental College, as Chairperson of the Mathematics Department, and as Director of Project Bridge, an integrated basic skills program that has been nationally recognized. Jacobs has served as a consultant to library literacy programs working on basic mathematics skills and with programs working with the deaf and other disabled people. He has also served on a State of California Work Team designing a State School-to-Work plan.

TONY Q. MARTINEZ has been teaching at Leander High School since 1982 and is currently the Mathematics Department Chair. During this time, he has implemented CORE Applied Mathematics and has served as a nationally recognized teacher trainer for the curriculum. Martinez has served on the Texas Education Agency's Item Review Committee for the Texas Assessment of Academic Skills and has most recently been selected as a Master Teacher for the National Teacher Training Institute for Math, Science, and Technology. He is currently a member of the Austin Area Council of Teachers of Mathematics, the Texas Council of Teacher of Mathematics, the Texas Association of Supervisors of Mathematics, and the National Council of Teachers of Mathematics.

PAMELA MATTHEWS is a faculty member at American University and was a community college instructor for 25 years. As an administrator at Mt. Hood Community College, she was the Principal Investigator of the National Science Foundation's Advanced Technological Education project, "An Application-Based, Technology-Supported, One-Track Mathematics Curriculum." She serves on the Mathematical Association of America's Committee on the Teaching of Undergraduate Mathematics and was a member of the National Council of Teachers of Mathematics and American Vocational Association's Joint Task Force on Mathematics and Vocational Education. She serves on the Executive Committee of the MSEB and on the National Advisory Committee of the Los Angeles Collaborative for Teacher Excellence, a National Science Foundation funded project. She was on the writing team of the National Research Council's publication, *Mathematics and Science Education Around the World: What Can We Learn from the Survey of Mathematics and Science Opportunities (SMSO) and the Third International Mathematics and Science Study (TIMSS)?*.

PATRICK MCCRAY is Systems Project Leader at G.D. Searle & Co., Monsanto. He is a member of the American Mathematical Society (AMS) Short Course Subcommittee and has served as Chair of the committee. He has served as Governor-At-Large on the Mathematical Association of America (MAA) Board of Governors, and as a member of the MAA Taskforce on Board Effectiveness. At the state level, he has served as Chair of the Illinois Section of the MAA and as Editor of its newsletter, *Greater than Zero*. In addition to belonging to the AMS and MAA, McCray is a member of the Association for Women in Mathematics, the Association for Computing Machinery, and the Institute of Electrical and Electronics Engineers' Computer Society.

KAREN DEE MICHALOWICZ has been in secondary education for 33 years. She is the Upper School Mathematics Chair at the Langley School in McLean, Virginia. In addition, she holds an Adjunct Faculty position at George Mason University. She is a Presidential Awardee for Excellence in Mathematics Teaching.

HENRY O. POLLAK was a research mathematician at Bell Laboratories for 32 years and an Assistant Vice-President at Bellcore for three years. He retired in 1986 and is now a visiting Professor of Mathematics Education at Teachers College, Columbia University.

JACK PRICE is Professor of Mathematics Education and Co-director of the Center for Education and Equity in Mathematics, Science, and Technology in the College of Science, California State Polytechnic University, Pomona. He is the immediate past President of the National Council of Teachers of Mathematics (NCTM).

ALAN H. SCHOENFELD is the Elizabeth and Edward Conner Professor of Education and Professor of Mathematics at the University of California, Berkeley. Schoenfeld's research is on mathematical thinking, teaching, and learning. He has focused on problem solving and assessment and is currently a writing group leader for the NCTM's Future of the Standards project, also called "Standards 2000."

DANIEL TEAGUE has recently served on the MSEB, on the Editorial Board of NCTM's Student Math Notes, as the technology consultant for the NCTM Secondary Level standards Addenda Projects, and as a member of NCTM's Commission on the Future of the Standards. From 1985 to 1991 and again in 1993, Mr. Teague served as Co-director of the Woodrow Wilson Summer Mathematics Institutes. Teague and Helen Compton are section editors of "Everybody's Problems" for the Consortium for Mathematics and Its Applications (COMAP).

INDEX

post-secondary education preparation, 93, 107–110

problem solving, 97, 98, 100, 103

standards, 60–62, 63–66, 95, 104, 107–108, 137

tasks, inclusion in, 94–95, 97–101, 104, 108–110, 138, 159

teaching, relationship to, 129–130, 132–133

testing, influence on, 61–62, 70–74

tracking, educational, 11, 12, 15, 24–29, 73

see also Tasks, mathematical, by content

Curriculum and Evaluation Standards for School Mathematics, 60, 65, 137

D

Data analysis, 4, 12, 21, 22, 68, 75

tasks, 16, 18–23, 27, 42–44, 56, 64, 71–74, 115–116, 153

see also Graphical representations and tables; Spreadsheets; Tasks, mathematical, by content

Data representation, *see* Graphical representations and tables

Department of Education, 3

Department of Energy, 56

Department of Labor, 3

Developmental education, 3, 15, 35, 36

Diagrams, *see* Graphical representations and tables

Discrete mathematics, 158

E

Economic factors, *see* Cost analysis; Employment and employers; Financial applications; Wages and salaries

The Education Imperative, 2

Employment and employers

academic/vocational tracking, 25

see also Business applications; Careers, preparation for; School-to-work experiences; Wages and salaries

Energy conservation, 13, 33, 54–56

Engineering, 3, 37–38, 47, 77

Environmental science, 27, 31, 32, 47, 49

Equity issues, 11, 73, 116

Error of measurement, 22, 119, 145, 146

Estimation, 12–13, 21, 30, 31, 76, 131, 145

tasks, 37–38, 45–48, 119–122, 123–126, 139, 145–146

Evaluation, *see* Assessment; Standards

Everybody Counts, ix, 9, 103

Exponential functions, 4, 76, 99, 109–110, 111

F

Federal government

assessments, 59, 62, 69, 73, 77–79

legislation, 3, 26, 29, 60

see also Carl Perkins Vocational and Technical Education Act; School-to-Work Opportunities Act of 1994; *headings beginning "Department of . . ."*

Fermi problems, *see* Estimation

Financial applications, 87–90, 98, 99, 105, 109–110, 111–114, 124–125, 133

Foreign countries, 18–23, 76–78

Formulae, 9, 16, 69, 81, 84–86, 87–88, 90, 112, 113, 117, 121–122, 146, 151

rules of thumb, 39, 95, 123–126

Fractals, 146

Functions, 22, 39, 40, 56, 75–76, 98–99, 110, 112–113, 158

concept of, 37

exponential, 4, 76, 99, 109–110, 111

linear, 33–34, 54–56, 78, 95, 98, 99, 105, 108, 113, 123–126, 133, 147–152, 158

quadratic, 32, 69, 95, 99, 121, 124

trigonometric, 12, 31, 75, 109

G

Gender issues, *see* Equity issues

Geometry

area calculations, 16, 38, 39, 47, 131, 145–146

curricular design, 95, 100, 104, 109

fractals, 146

representation, 65, 77, 95, 117–118, 119–122, 147–152

mapmaking, 110, 146

ordered pairs, 95, 120

tasks, 39, 64–65, 76, 77, 109, 110, 117–118, 119–122, 145–146, 147–152, 158

topology, 104

vectors, 95, 117–118

Germany, 76

The Goals 2000: Educate America Act, 29(n.5), 60

Government role, *see* Federal government; State government

Graphical representations and tables, 30, 37, 76, 108, 133–134

algebra, 39–40, 55, 80–82, 87–90, 105, 109–110, 111–114, 124, 133

data analysis, 12, 21, 42–44, 115–116, 153

geometry, 65, 77, 95, 117–118, 119–122, 147–152

modeling, 49–53, 55

Problem solving, 1, 3, 10–11, 12, 16, 27–28, 31, 79, 132
   assessment of, 61
   business/marketing application, 18–23
   classroom environment, 139
   curricular design, 97, 98, 100, 103
   difficulty level, 138, 139
   mental mathematics, 83–84
   research support for problem-centered teaching, 11, 73
   skills, relationship with, 59, 95, 97, 103
   standards, 60, 61, 64, 68
   teacher involvement, 130, 132–140
   theory, relationship with, 103
   types of problems, 98–99
   see also Algorithms and procedures; Open-ended problems; Word problems; *headings beginning "Tasks . . ."*
Procedures, *see* Algorithms and procedures; Conceptual understanding
Professional education, *see* Teacher education
Professional Standards for Teaching Mathematics, 130
Proportional reasoning, 4, 38, 54–56, 78, 94, 104, 115–118
Psychological factors, *see* Motivation

Q
Quadratic functions, 32, 69, 95, 99, 121, 124

R
Rates, 62, 78, 80–82, 87–90, 95, 100, 110, 111–114, 115–118, 147–152
Reasoning, *see* Conceptual understanding; Habits of mind; Mental mathematics; Problem solving
Recursion, 62, 75, 76, 80–82, 87–90, 105, 111–114
Remedial education, *see* Developmental education
Research
   science/math integration, 64
   supporting problem-centered teaching, 11, 73
Reshaping School Mathematics, ix, 10
Rote learning, *see* Memorization
Rounding off, 76, 90, 95, 119–122
Rules of thumb, 39, 95, 123–126

S
Salaries, *see* Wages and salaries
Sampling, 19–20, 22, 44
SAT, 61, 71–74

SCANS, *see* Secretary's Commission on Achieving Necessary Skills
Scholastic Aptitude Test, *see* SAT
School-to-work experiences, 3, 10, 12–13, 26–27
   algebra, role in, 2, 12, 35–41, 94
   interdisciplinary collaboration, 26, 27
   sources of, 164
   see also Tasks, mathematical, by context
School-to-Work Opportunities Act of 1994, 3, 26
Science education, 10, 47
   basis for careers, 1, 9, 12, 30, 34
   mathematics, relationship with, 3, 24, 25–27, 31, 75–77
   standards, 60, 63–66
   tasks, 64–65, 80–82
   TIMSS, 4, 95
Secretary's Commission on Achieving Necessary Skills, 60–61, 67–69
Simpson's paradox, 95
Skills, *see* Algorithms and procedures; Communication skills; Conceptual understandings; Memorization
Spreadsheets, 32, 68, 80–82, 87–90, 94–95, 103, 105, 111–112, 133, 153, 158
Standards, 3, 59–90
   academic/vocational education integrated, 28
   assessments, relation to, 59, 61, 141–144
   calculus, 28
   communication skills, 60, 62, 64, 66, 68, 69, 78–79, 137
   curricular design, 60–62, 63–66, 95, 104, 107–108, 137
   definitional issues, 60
   national, 59, 61
   National Skills Standards Board, 29(n.5), 60
   NCTM, 28, 61, 63–64, 137
   NSES, 60, 64–66
   parents' role in standardized testing, 61, 70, 74
   problem solving, 60, 61, 63–64, 68, 130, 137–138
   SCANS, 60–61, 67–69
   State government role, 59, 60
   teaching methods, 130, 137–140, 142
   technical education, 2
   see also Assessment; Curriculum and curricular design
State government
   assessment and standards, 59, 60
   local support for teachers, 130
State-to-state comparisons, SAT testing, 71–74
Statistics, 4, 74, 75, 100, 115–116, 158
   sampling, 19–20, 22, 44

tasks, 18–23, 42–44
see also Data analysis; Estimation;
Probability
Successive approximation, 75, 145

T

Tables and charts, *see* Graphical
representations and tables
Tasks, mathematical, 4, 9
curriculum, selection of, 94–95, 97–101, 104,
108–110, 138, 159
source of, 163–166
see also Open-ended problems; Problem
solving; Tasks, mathematical, by content;
Tasks, mathematical, by context
Tasks, mathematical, by content, 4, 9
algebra, 32, 33–34, 54–56, 76, 80–82,
83–86, 87–90, 98, 99, 100, 109–110,
111–114, 117, 118, 121–122, 123–124,
133, 158
calculus, 54–56, 121–122, 145–146
data collection and analysis, 16, 18–23, 27,
42–44, 56, 71–74, 115–116, 153
estimation, 37–38, 45–48, 119–122, 123–126,
139, 145–146
fractals, 146
geometry, 39, 64–65, 76, 77, 109, 110,
117–118, 119–122, 145–146, 147–152, 158
optimization, 49–53
probability, 21, 76, 115–118, 119–122, 158
proportional reasoning, 38, 54–56, 78,
115–118
rates, 78, 80–82, 87–90, 100, 110, 111–114,
115–118, 147–152
recursion, 80–82, 87–90, 105, 111–114
representation, 39–40, 42–44, 49–53,
109–110, 115–118, 119–122, 133, 147–152
statistics, 18–23, 42–44
vectors, 117–118
weighted averages, 115–118
see also Functions; Open-ended problems;
School-to-work experiences; Spreadsheets
Tasks, mathematical, by context
agriculture, 39
automobiles, 105, 123–124, 125–126, 140,
147–152, 153
baseball, 116, 158
body proportions, 125, 145–146
business, 18–23, 45, 46–47, 49–53, 76, 83,
84–86, 119–121
construction, 37–38, 39, 109
cooking, 125
energy conservation, 33, 54–56
environmental science, 27, 31, 32, 47, 49

finance, 87–90, 98, 99, 105, 109–110,
111–114, 124–125, 133
health care, 39–40, 42–44, 80–82, 115–118,
145–146
hypothetical, 139
mapmaking, 110, 146
mathematics, 76, 77, 83, 84, 105, 121–122,
158
piano tuning, 45
police protection, 47
salaries, 45, 115, 116
school and education, 16, 33–34, 45, 46,
71–74, 116–117
science, 64–65, 80–82
tax, 47–48, 78, 99, 125
wages and salaries, 45, 115, 116
Tax calculations, 47–48, 78, 99, 125
Taxonomy of Educational Objectives, 97
Teacher education, 3, 4, 127–153
inservice teachers, 141–144
preservice teachers, 130, 134–135, 137, 139
Teachers, 3, 4
assessment, involvement in, 130, 141–144
attitudes, 134, 140
communication skills, 134, 139–140
local support for, 130
motivation, 134–135, 136, 140, 142–143
problem solving, 132–140
student interactions, 10, 129, 135–136,
139–140
Teaching, 3, 14–15, 129–153
curricular design, 129–130, 132–133
feedback, 129, 139
interdisciplinary collaboration, 26, 27
memorization, 15, 95, 134
standards, 63–64, 130, 137–140, 142
see also Curriculum and curricular design;
Group learning; Memorization; Models
and modeling; Problem solving; Tasks,
mathematical
Technical applications, *see* Tasks, mathematical,
by context
Technical education, 2, 3, 164
Tests and testing, *see* Assessment
Theory, relationship with problem solving, 103
Third International Mathematics and Science
Study, 4, 95
TIMSS, *see* Third International Mathematics
and Science Study
Tracking, vocational/academic, 11, 12, 15,
24–29, 73
Trigonometry, 12, 31, 75, 109
Two-year colleges, 2, 3, 15, 26, 27, 29, 60, 140,
164

U

Uncertainty, 20, 21, 23, 25
  error of measurement, 22, 119, 145, 146
Universities and colleges, *see* Post-secondary
  education; Two-year colleges
University of Chicago School Mathematics
  Project, 99

V

VATEA, *see* Carl Perkins Vocational and
  Technical Education Act
Vectors, 95, 117–118
Visual aids, *see* Graphical representations and
  tables

Vocational education, 2, 109, 164
  academic education and, 11, 12, 15, 24–29, 164
  see also Technical education

W

Wages and salaries, 26
  tasks, 45, 115, 116
Weighted averages, 115–118
What Work Requires of Schools, 60, 67, 68–69
Word problems, 15, 32–33, 69, 98, 108
  see also Tasks, mathematical, by content;
    Tasks, mathematical, by context
Workplace, *see* Careers, preparation for;
    Employment and employers; School-to-
    work experiences